CW00401998
BOURBON
MADRID
See pp26–37
0 metres 1000
0 yards 1000

EYEWITNESS TRAVEL

MADRID

POCKET GUIDE

PROJECT DIRECTORS Nicholas Bevan, Derek Hall
EDITORS Derek Hall, Marion Dent, Sue Juby
DESIGNER Tony Truscott
INDEXER Michael Dent
PICTURE RESEARCHER Mirco De Cet
CARTOGRAPHY John Plumer

Conceived and produced by Redback Publishing, 25 Longhope Drive, Farnham, Surrey, GU10 4SN

Printed and bound in China

First published in Great Britain in 2006
by Dorling Kindersley Limited
80 Strand, London WC2R 0RL

17 18 19 20 10 9 8 7 6 5 4 3 2 1

Reprinted with revisions 2008, 2010, 2012, 2014, 2018

A CIP CATALOGUE RECORD IS AVAILABLE FROM THE BRITISH LIBRARY.

ISBN: 978-0-24131-031-1

The information in this
DK Eyewitness Travel Guide is checked regularly.

Every effort has been made to ensure that this book is as up-to-date as possible at the time of going to press. Some details, however, such as telephone numbers, opening hours, prices, gallery hanging arrangements and travel information, are liable to change. The publishers cannot accept responsibility for any consequences arising from the use of this book, nor for any material on third-party websites, and cannot guarantee that any website address in this book will be a suitable source of travel information. We value the views and suggestions of our readers highly. Please write to:
Publisher, DK Eyewitness Travel Guides,
Dorling Kindersley, 80 Strand, London WC2R 0RL.

The Neo-Classical Museo del Prado

from the excesses of Baroque *(see p34)*.

Parks and Gardens

Parque del Retiro
Once a royal playground, now a huge green park for tourists and *Madrileños* alike (*see p35*).

Real Jardín Botánico
A stunning collection of plants from the Philippines and South America can be found here (*see p36*).

Campo del Moro
A steep, green park rising up in the old town, giving fabulous views of the Palacio Real (*see p23*).

Estación de Atocha
An extraordinary indoor palm garden can be found in the original old railway station (*see p37*).

Palacio Real de Aranjuez
Take a cool walk in the gardens of the royal summer

Palacio Real de Aranjuez

palace, while eating strawberries and asparagus in season (*see p67*).

Tabernas

La Venencia
Established over 70 years ago, this typically Spanish taberna serves the best sherry (*see p25*).

A tiled Madrid taberna

Viva Madrid
Famous for its fine ceramic work, this *taberna* has been adopted by the younger *Madrileño* crowd around the lively Plaza de Santa Ana area (*see p25*).

Taberna de Antonio Sánchez
Madrid's *tabernas* take their cue from this 180-year-old watering hole (*see p25*).

La Bola
This small *taberna* was founded 140 years ago. It has a beautifully carved wooden bar and serves some of Madrid's best *cocido* (*see p25*).

Sobrino de Botín
Established in 1725, this is reputed to be the world's oldest restaurant. It serves traditional Castilian fare like roast lamb (*see p25*).

Plaza de Chueca
The exquisitely decorated Bodega de Angel Sierra bar has hardly changed since it was built in 1897 (see p40).

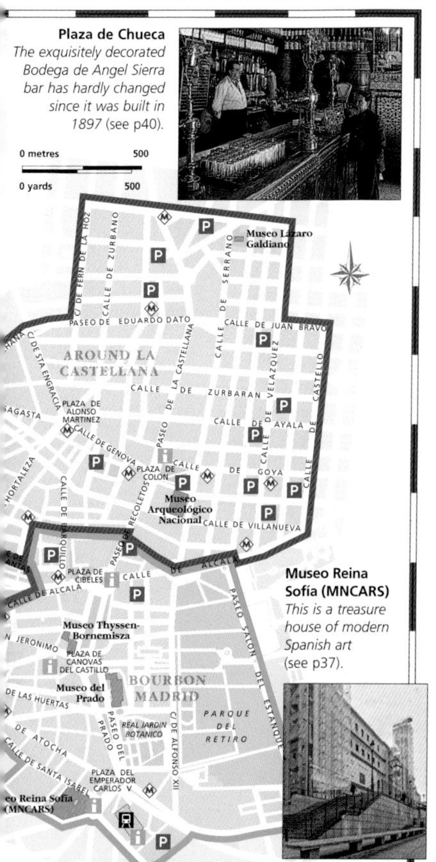

Museo Reina Sofía (MNCARS)
This is a treasure house of modern Spanish art (see p37).

Plaza de Cibeles
One of Madrid's best-known landmarks, and also one of the most beautiful (see p29).

Madrid's Highlights

If you only have limited time to spend in Madrid, the following highlights are designed to help you see the best of what is on offer and to ensure you get the maximum enjoyment from this fascinating, multilayered ancient and modern city.

Museums and Galleries

Museo Arqueológico Nacional

Museo Arqueológico Nacional
Second only to the Museo del Prado, this extensively refurbished museum has exhibits dating from prehistoric times to the 19th century *(see p42).*

Museo del Prado
Recognized as one of the world's great art galleries, the Prado is particularly notable for its collections by Velázquez and Goya. It also boasts paintings by masters such as Rubens, Raphael, Titian and Tintoretto *(see p34).*

Museo Reina Sofía (MNCARS)
An outstanding collection of 20th-century art including *Retrato de Josette*, by Juan Gris, and *Guernica*, Picasso's famous Civil War protest painting *(see p37).*

Museo Thyssen-Bornemisza
A vast private collection tracing Western art through the ages, with major works by Titian, Goya, Picasso and Rubens *(see p31).*

Museo Lázaro Galdiano
occupies an elegant Neo-Renaissance mansion and has an eclectic collection of artworks ranging from the 6th century BC to the 20th century *(see p43).*

Architecture

Bourbon
The French-influenced grand Puerta de Alcalá was erected by Carlos III as part of his plan to improve eastern Madrid *(see p28).*

Baroque
The Palacio Real, Madrid's fabulous Royal Palace, was inspired by Bernini's designs for the Louvre in Paris *(see pp18–21).*

Habsburg
The Monasterio de las Descalzas Reales has been home to a society of cloistered nuns with Habsburg lineage – the Royal Barefoot Sisters *(see p16).*

Art Deco
The Gran Vía has many fine Art Deco buildings, including the Palacio de la Música *(see p13).*

Neo-Classical
Museo del Prado exemplifies the Neo-Classical move towards dignity and away

Monument of Alfonso XII (1901) in the Parque del Retiro

CONTENTS

INTRODUCING MADRID

Central Madrid **4**

Madrid's Highlights **6**

MADRID AREA BY AREA

Old Madrid **8**

Bourbon Madrid **26**

Around La Castellana **38**

Further Afield **46**

Beyond Madrid **52**

PRACTICAL INFORMATION

Getting Around **74**

Survival Guide **76**

Index **78**

Acknowledgments **80**

Interior of La Casa del Abuelo

A winged statue at the entrance to the Museo Arqueologicó

Central Madrid

Madrid is the capital of Spain, and is located more or less in the centre of the country. There are three main areas of the city, all dazzling with their own style: Old Madrid, still visibly linked to its Moorish past, Bourbon Madrid, which reflects the city's dynastic links with France, and Castellana, the modern sector.

Plaza de Colón
This large square is a monument to Christopher Columbus (see p42).

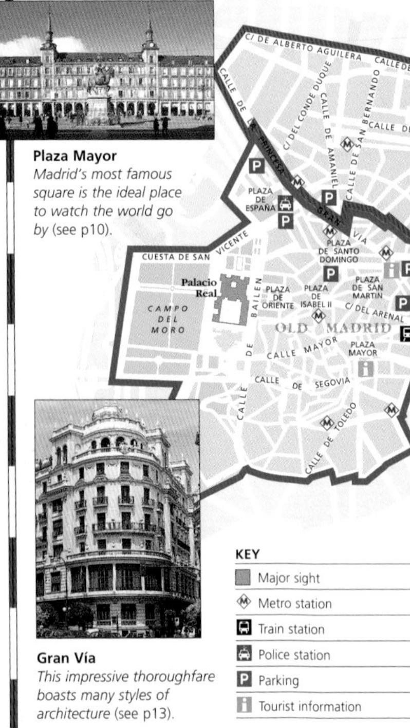

Plaza Mayor
Madrid's most famous square is the ideal place to watch the world go by (see p10).

Gran Vía
This impressive thoroughfare boasts many styles of architecture (see p13).

OLD MADRID

Stretching from the Plaza de la Villa to the busy Puerta del Sol, the compact centre of Old Madrid is steeped in history and full of interesting sights. At its heart is the vast square, the Plaza Mayor.

SIGHTS AT A GLANCE

Historic Buildings
Muralla Árabe 24
Palacio de Santa Cruz 7
Palacio del Senado 16
Palacio Real pp18–21 18
Teatro Real 20
Telefónica 11

Museums and Galleries
Real Academia de Bellas Artes de San Fernando 9

Churches and Convents
Basílica Pontificia de San Miguel 5
Catedral de la Almudena 22
Colegiata de San Isidro 6
Iglesia de San Nicolás 21
Monasterio de la Encarnación 17
Monasterio de las Descalzas Reales 13
San Francisco el Grande 25

Streets, Squares, Parks and Districts
Calle de Preciados 14
Campo del Moro 23
Gran Vía 10
La Latina 27
Plaza de España 15
Plaza de la Paja 26
Plaza de la Villa 4
Plaza de Oriente 19
Plaza de Santa Ana 8
Plaza del Callao 12
Plaza Mayor 2
Puerta del Sol 1

Markets
El Rastro 28
Mercado de San Miguel 3

KEY
Metro station
Train station
Main bus stop
Tourist information

SEE ALSO
• *Street Life p25*

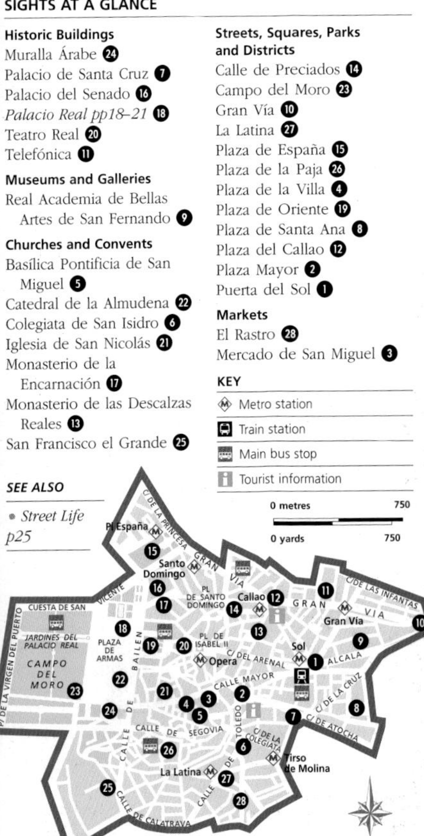

◀ *Side street with a view of the Colegiata de San Isidro, Plaza Mayor*

Kilometre Zero, the centre of Spain's road network

Puerta del Sol ❶

Map E5.

The bustling Puerta del Sol ("Gateway of the Sun") is one of Madrid's most popular meeting places. It marks the site of the original eastern entrance to Madrid. In the late 19th century the area was turned into a square and became the centre of café society. Today the "square" is shaped like a half moon. Its southern side is occupied by the austere red-brick Casa de Correos, home to the regional government. Outside the building, a symbol on the ground marks Kilometre Zero, considered the centre of Spain's road network. A railway station now connects "Sol" with the northern Chamartín station and the southern Atocha station. At midnight on New Year's Eve crowds fill the square and people swallow a grape on each stroke of the clock, hoping to bring good luck for the new year.

Plaza Mayor ❷

Map D5.

The Plaza Mayor forms a splendid public space. Construction began in 1617, at the order of Felipe III, and was completed in just two years, replacing slum houses on the site. An equestrian statue of Felipe III stands in the centre. The fanciest part of the arcaded construction is the Casa de la Panadería (bakery). Nowadays the square is lined with outdoor cafés and is the venue for a collectors' market on Sundays. The southern exit leads into the Calle de Toledo towards El Rastro, Madrid's famous flea market (*see p24*). A flight of steps in the southwest corner of the square takes you under the Arco de Cuchilleros to the Calle de Cuchilleros, where there are a number of *mesones*, or traditional restaurants.

Allegorical paintings decorate the Casa de la Panadería, Plaza Mayor

Mercado de San Miguel ❸

Map D5. Plaza de San Miguel. Open 10am–midnight Sun–Wed, 10am–2am Thu–Sat.

This unique single-level, glassed-in market was built in 1914–15, and is the last surviving example in the capital of a marketplace

Shopping arcade of the renowned San Miguel Market

constructed from iron. Now the market is filled with various delicatessen stalls and bars. However, it can get very crowded at night.

Plaza de la Villa ❹

Map C5.

This much restored and remodelled square is surrounded by many historic buildings. The façade on Calle de Sacramento is an excellent example of the Plateresque style – early Spanish Renaissance with fine detail. Linked to this building by a bridge is the town hall (*ayuntamiento*), designed in the 1640s by Juan Gómez de Mora, architect of the Plaza Mayor. A balcony was later added so that the royal family could watch Corpus Christi processions passing by.

Basílica Pontificia de San Miguel ❺

Map C5. Calle de San Justo 4. Open daily. Free.

Standing on the site of an old Romanesque church dedicated to two local child-martyrs put to death by the Romans, this building is a rare example of Bourbon-inspired Baroque. It was built for Don Luis de Borbón y Farnesio, the youngest son of Felipe V and Archbishop of Toledo at only five years of age.

Colegiata de San Isidro ❻

Map D6. Calle Toledo 37. Open daily. Free.

This church was built in the Baroque style for Jesuits in the mid-17th century. In 1767 it was rededicated to St Isidore, Madrid's patron saint, and some years later the saint's remains were brought here from the Iglesia de San Andrés. The Colegiata was returned to the Jesuits in the reign of Fernando VII (1814–33).

Statue of Charity on the façade of Basílica Pontificia de San Miguel

The 17th-century Palacio de Santa Cruz – a jewel of Habsburg architecture

Palacio de Santa Cruz 7

Map D5. Plaza de Santa Cruz. Closed to the public.

Constructed between 1629 and 1643, this building is one of the jewels of Habsburg architecture. Since 1901 it has been the Ministry of Foreign Affairs, but it has also housed the Overseas Ministry, law courts and, originally, the Carcel de la Corte (city prison). The famous bandit Luis Candelas spent his last hours in its cells. (One of Madrid's tourist restaurants, situated on nearby Cava de San Miguel, is named after him.)

Plaza de Santa Ana 8

Map E5.

This large pedestrian square is a popular gathering place with a lively atmosphere. Monuments to two of Spain's most famous writers testify to the square's strong literary connections. At one end is a statue of the poet Federico García Lorca (1899–1936); at the other is the marble figure of Pedro Calderón de la Barca (1600–81). The terraces of Plaza de Santa Ana and adjoining streets are home to some of the city's most popular bars and restaurants. The classic Cervecería Alemana, built in 1904 and once frequented by Ernest Hemingway, is always packed. Around the corner from Teatro Español *(see p33)* is the Viva Madrid, a popular bar with young singles.

Scene from a play by Calderón de la Barca adorning his statue

Real Academia de Bellas Artes de San Fernando 9

Map E5. Calle de Alcalá 13. Open 10am–3pm Tue–Sun except some public hols. Adm charge. Free Wed.

Dalí and Picasso are among the former students of this arts academy, housed in an 18th-century building by Churriguera. Its art gallery displays a large selection of works, including drawings by Raphael and Titian and paintings by Rubens, Van Dyck, El Greco, Velázquez and Goya, a former director.

Gran Vía ⑩

Map E4.

With its eclectic architecture, this is the city's most impressive thoroughfare. On the drawing board since 1860, the project was inaugurated in 1908 but not finished until 1929. The new street gave architects an opportunity to prove their skill, providing a survey of early 20th-century design trends, including some of the best examples of modern architecture in the city. The magnificent Edificio Grassy, built in 1917, is home to a prestigious jewellery company. Today's Gran Vía continues to be a throbbing main artery for the city, lined with theatres and cinemas, shops, hotels and restaurants.

Gran Via, the main shopping street in Madrid

The skyscraper-styled Telefónica

Telefónica ⑪

Map E4. Gran Vía.

This American-designed building, was inspired by Manhattan's skyscrapers. Built between 1926 and 1929 to house the Spanish telephone company, the Telefónica was Madrid's tallest building. Its façade consists of tapered setbacks, ending in a central tower 81 m (266 ft) tall. The architect added the exterior ornamentation to make it look similar to the neighbouring buildings. It also hosts de Telefonica Foundation, an art and digital culture exhibition centre.

Plaza del Callao ⑫

Map D4.

At the junction of Gran Vía and Calle de Preciados is the Plaza del Callao. This used to be the movie mecca of Madrid. The Art Deco Callao and Capitol cinemas (built in 1927 and 1933 respectively) still remain, while others have been converted into boutiques and theatres.

Night-time traffic on the Gran Vía, seen from the Plaza de España ▶

HOTEL WASHINGTO

VP

Chapel with ornate altar in the Monasterio de las Descalzas Reales

Monasterio de las Descalzas Reales ⓭

Map D5. Plaza de las Descalzas. Open Tue–Sun, public hols. Closed 1, 6 Jan, 12–15 Apr, 1 May, 24, 25, 31 Dec. Adm charge. Free Wed & Thu afternoons for EU residents.

Madrid's most notable religious building is also a rare surviving example of 16th-century architecture in the city. Around 1560 Felipe II's sister Doña Juana converted the medieval palace which stood here into a convent for nuns and women of the royal household. Her rank, and that of her fellow nuns, accounts for the vast store of art and wealth of the *Descalzas Reales* (Royal Barefoot Sisters). There are works by Brueghel the Elder, Titian, Zurbarán, Murillo and Ribera. The main chapel houses Doña Juana's tomb.

Calle de Preciados ⓮

Map D5.

This pedestrian street leading north from Puerta del Sol to the Plaza de Callao is now the domain of shoppers. Calle de Preciados acquired its modern look during the *Ensanche* (urban renewal) of the mid-19th century. It is the birthplace of Spain's most successful department store chain, El Corte Inglés. At the north end of the street is the local branch of the French FNAC chain, as well as a beautiful bookshop and café, La Central. Trendy boutiques and old-fashioned shops share the space between them.

Plaza de España ⓯

Map C4.

One of Madrid's busiest traffic intersections and most popular meeting places, Plaza de España acquired its present appearance during the Franco period with the construction of the massive Edificio España which is closed for restoration. Commissioned by the Metropolitana real

Stone obelisk with statue of Cervantes, Plaza de España

estate developers, the 26-floor concrete structure was built between 1947 and 1953. Metropolitana also built the 33-floor Torre de Madrid on the corner of Plaza de España and Calle Princesa, completed in 1957 and nicknamed *La Jirafa* (the Giraffe). At the centre of this square is a massive stone obelisk built in 1928. In front of it is a statue of Miguel de Cervantes *(see p66)*.

Old assembly hall of the Palacio del Senado

Palacio del Senado ⓰

Map C4. Plaza de la Marina Española 8. Weekday tours by appt (tel 91 538 13 75 or email: visitas@senado.es). Closed Easter, Aug, public hols. Free.

The upper house of the Cortes (Spanish parliament) is installed in a 16th-century monastery, adapted in 1814 for the purpose. It became the Senate headquarters 23 years later. In 1991 a modern granite-and-glass, circular wing was added at the back of the building to make more space. The Palacio del Senado is open to the public for three days in December each year, to commemorate the establishment of the Constitution on 6 December.

Monasterio de la Encarnación ⓱

Map C4. Plaza de la Encarnación. Open Tue–Sun, public hols. Closed 1, 6 Jan, 12–15 Apr, 1 May, 24, 25, 31 Dec. Adm charge. Free Wed & Thu afternoons for EU residents.

Set in a tree-shaded square, this Augustinian convent was founded in 1611 for Margaret of Austria, wife of Felipe III. Still inhabited by nuns, the convent has the atmosphere of Old Castile, with Talavera tiles, exposed beams and portraits of royal benefactors. It also contains a collection of 17th- and 18th-century art, with paintings by José de Ribera and Vincente Carducho. The main attraction is the reliquary chamber, used to store the bones of saints. There is also a phial of St Pantaleon's dried blood which, according to legend, liquifies every 27 July, the saint's birthday.

Imposing entrance to the Monasterio de la Encarnación

Palacio Real ⓲

See pp18–21.

Palacio Real 18

The site of Madrid's vast and lavish Royal Palace had been occupied by a fortress but, after a fire in 1734, Felipe V commissioned a palatial replacement. The Palace was used by the royal family until the abdication of Alfonso XIII in 1931. It is now used for state occasions.

The Dining Room *evokes the grandeur of Bourbon and Habsburg entertaining.*

The Porcelain Room *is entirely covered in royal Buen Retiro porcelain.*

The Gasparini Room *is decorated with lavish Rococo chinoiserie.*

VISITORS' CHECKLIST

Map B5. Calle de Bailén. Open Apr–Sep: 10am–8pm daily; Oct–Mar: 10am–6pm daily. Closed 1, 6 Jan, 1 May, 31 Dec. Adm charge. Free Apr–Sep: Mon–Thu from 6pm (Oct–Mar: from 4pm) for EU residents.
www.patrimonionacional.es

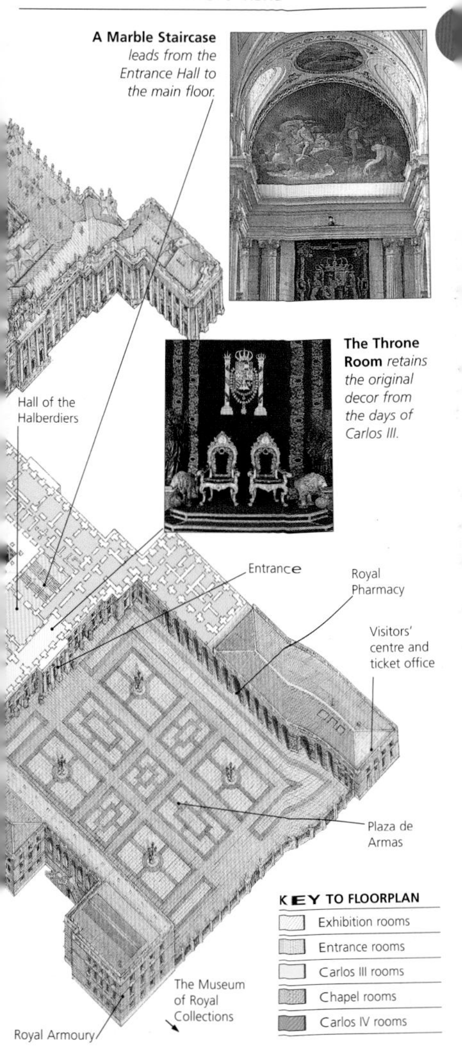

A Marble Staircase *leads from the Entrance Hall to the main floor.*

The Throne Room *retains the original decor from the days of Carlos III.*

Exploring the Palacio Real

This splendid Royal Palace stands on the site of the original Moorish fortress, or Alcázar, which served as a residence for visiting royals after the Christian conquest of Madrid in 1085. The alcázar was destroyed by fire on Christmas Eve, 1734, during the reign of Felipe V. This suited Spain's first Bourbon king well – his idea of a royal palace was the Versailles of his childhood, and so he commissioned a new royal palace decorated in the French style.

The Palace

Most of the massive limestone and granite building is the work of Italian Giovanni Battista Sachetti. So vast was the plan that construction lasted from 1738 to 1764, by which time Felipe V was dead. His son, Carlos III, became the first royal resident. Visitors enter the palace from the Plaza de Armas.

Entrance Rooms

The Toledo marble in the main stairway provides a regal taste of what follows. The first port of call is the Salón de los Alabarderos (Hall of the Halberdiers, or palace guards), decorated with a fresco by Tiépolo. Adjoining it is the Salón de Columnas (Hall of Columns), which served as the banquet hall until the new dining hall was incorporated in the 19th century. Visitors enter the Carlos III rooms through the 18th-century Rococo Salón del Trono (Throne Room), whose decor has remained constant throughout generations of rulers.

Throne Room, Carlos III Rooms

Carlos III Rooms

Leading off from the Throne Room are three smaller halls named after Mattia Gasparini, the original decorator. These were the king's private chambers. He would take his meals in the Sala de Gasparini and be dressed in the Cámara de Gasparini. The walls of the Baroque Sala de Porcelana (Porcelain Room) are covered by 18th-century porcelain from the Buen Retiro factory. The Salita Amarilla (Yellow Room) gets its name from the tapestry covering its walls.

Plaza de Armas. The square forms the entrance to the Royal Pharmacy

Dining Room

This 400-sq m (4,300-sq ft) banquet hall was formed in 1879 when the queen's private chambers were joined together during the reign of Alfonso XII. It is richly adorned with gold plate decoration, frescoes, chandeliers, Flemish tapestries, Chinese vases and embroidered curtains. The table can accommodate up to 160 diners.

Chapel Rooms

Built in 1749–57, the chapel is still used for religious services, and also for musical soirées. While the decor is luxurious, it is the dome, with its murals by Giaquinto, which immediately catches the eye. Next, visitors pass through the Salón de Paso and into María Cristina's chambers. During the reign of Alfonso XII these four small rooms served several functions.

Pharmacy and Armoury

Returning to the Plaza de Armas, near the ticket office is the Real Farmacia (Royal Pharmacy) founded by Felipe II in 1594. The pharmacy is a warren of rooms, with jars and vials bearing the names of potions and medicinal plants. On the other side of the plaza is the Real Armería (Royal Armoury), in a pavilion built in 1897. It could be considered as Madrid's first museum, because it has been open to the public since Felipe II inherited the collection from his father. On display is a suit of armour worn by Carlos I, the Holy Roman Emperor Charles V.

Herb drawer in the Pharmacy

Equestrian statue of Felipe IV by Pietro Tacca, Plaza de Oriente

Plaza de Oriente 19

Map C5.

During his days as king of Spain, Joseph Bonaparte (José I) carved out this stirrup-shaped space from the jumble of buildings to the east of the Palacio Real *(see pp18–21)*. The many statues of early kings which stand here were originally intended to adorn the roofline of the Palacio Real, but proved to be too heavy. The equestrian statue of Felipe IV in the centre of the square is by Italian sculptor Pietro Tacca, and is based on drawings made by Velázquez. In the southeast corner of the plaza is the Café de Oriente, with outdoor tables for enjoying the view.

Teatro Real 20

Map C5. Plaza de Oriente 5. Open for guided tours daily 10:30am–1pm every 30 minutes, except Aug. Adm charge.

Madrid's opera house stands opposite the Palacio Real *(see pp18–21)* on the Plaza de Oriente. It is an imposing six-sided grey building, made all the more impressive by the six floors below street level as well as the nine floors visible above ground. The second-floor restaurant is worth seeing. It has a ceiling representing Madrid's starlit sky as it was on the night of the theatre's inauguration. On the sixth floor there is a pleasant cafeteria which has a good view overlooking the

Awe-inspiring interior of Madrid's opera house, the Teatro Real

Plaza de Oriente and the Palacio Real. The Opera House took 32 years to build and was finished in 1850. However, much of the structure that exists today is the result of a massive renovation project which took place between 1991 and 1997. Like the original building programme, it was plagued with problems, and when it finally opened in October 1997 with a performance of Falla's *The Three-Cornered Hat,* it was five years behind schedule and way over budget.

Iglesia de San Nicolás ㉑

Map C5. Plaza de San Nicolás. Open 8:30–9:30am & 6:30–8:30pm daily. Free.

The brick tower of the church of San Nicolás de Bari, decorated with horse-shoe arches, is the oldest surviving religious structure in Madrid. Thought to date from the 12th century, it is Mudéjar in style, and may originally have been the minaret of a mosque.

12th-century Mudéjar-style brick tower of the Iglesia de San Nicolás

Catedral de la Almudena ㉒

Map B5. Calle de Bailén 10. Open 10am–9pm (museum closed Sun). Mass noon, 6pm, 8pm. Adm charge.

Work on Madrid's cathedral began in 1879 and only finished in 1993. The crypt houses a 16th-century statue of the Virgen de la Almudena.

View of the Catedral de la Almudena and the Palacio Real

Campo del Moro ㉓

Map B5. Paseo Virgen del Puerto. Open 10am–8pm Apr–Sep, 10am–6pm Oct–Mar. Closed 11 May, 12 Oct, 25 Dec. Free.

The Campo del Moro (Field of the Moor) rises steeply from the Río Manzanares to offer one of the finest views of the Palacio Real *(see pp18–21)*. In 1109, a Moorish army led by Ali ben Yusuf set up camp here – hence the name. In 1931, the park opened to the public, but closed again during the Civil War, not reopening until 1978.

Muralla Árabe ㉔

Map B5. Parque del Emir Mohamed I, Cuesta de la Vega. Open daily. Free.

Other than the city's name, which comes from the Arabic word *Mayrit*, a small stretch of outer defence wall is all that is left of Madrid's Moorish heritage. During the summer, outdoor concerts and plays are held in Parque del Emir Mohamed I.

San Francisco el Grande ㉕

Map B6. Plaza de San Francisco. Museum open Tue–Fri, Sat am (daily in Aug). Main chapel open Sat am. Adm charge (includes guided tour).

Built between 1760–84 on the site of a convent, this basilica was extravagantly renovated in 1878. It contains works by great artists and boasts the largest dome in Spain. The adjoining Capilla del Cristo de los Dolores dates from 1162.

San Francisco el Grande, endowed with work by great artists

Plaza de la Paja ㉖

Map C6.

Once the focus of medieval Madrid, the area around the Plaza de la Paja – literally Straw Square – is still atmospheric. Nearby is a cluster of interlinked squares, ending in the Plaza Puerta de Moros, a reminder of the Muslim community which once occupied the area.

The atmospheric Plaza de la Paja

La Latina ㉗

Map C6.

La Latina's steep streets are lined with tall, narrow houses. It offers plenty of taverns and is popular with a young crowd. The district of La Latina, together with the adjacent Lavapiés, is seen as the heart of *castizo* (traditional working-class) Madrid.

El Rastro ㉘

Map D6. Calle de la Ribera de Curtidores. Open 10am–2pm Sun, public hols.

Madrid's celebrated flea market, established in the Middle Ages, has its hub in the Plaza de Cascorro. The main street is the Calle de la Ribera de Curtidores, or "Tanners' Riverbank". The lively crowds and the vast array of goods in El Rastro make it an ideal way to spend a Sunday morning.

STREET LIFE

RESTAURANTS

La Venencia
Map E5. Calle Echegaray 7.
Tel 91 429 73 13.
Cheap
Popular with both locals and tourists for the five Spanish sherries on offer, this old taberna also has good tapas.

La Bola
Map C4. Calle de la Bola 5.
Tel 91 547 69 30. Closed Sun pm, Jul–Aug: Sat pm & Sun.
Moderate
La Bola has an original 19th-century dining room. The speciality is cocido, *served in earthenware pots* (pucheros). *Credit cards not accepted.*

Casa Ciriaco
Map C5. Calle Mayor 84.
Tel 91 548 06 20. Closed Aug.
Moderate
A good place to try classics such as the dessert bizcocho borracho *("cross-eyed drunk" – sponge cake soaked in wine and syrup).*

Sobrino de Botín
Map D5. Calle de los Cuchilleros 17. Tel 91 366 42 17.
Expensive
Writer Ernest Hemingway was a fan of this restaurant. His favourite dish, roast suckling pig, is still a house speciality.

BARS AND CAFÉS

Café de Oriente
Map C5. Plaza de Oriente 2.
Elegant café with velvet seats, stucco ceiling and terrace.

Casa Alberto
Map E6. Calle de las Huertas 18.
Closed Sun.
Cervantes wrote part of Don Quixote *at this historic tavern.*

La Casa del Abuelo
Map E5. Calle de la Victoria 12.
This tapas *bar* par excellence *was founded in 1906. The house speciality is prawns.*

Chocolatería San Ginés
Map D5. Pasadizo de S Ginés 5.
Head here after a night on the town for a traditional breakfast of chocolate con churros.

Taberna de Antonio Sánchez
Map D6. Calle de Mesón de Paredes 13. Closed Sun pm.
This atmospheric tavern serves interesting tapas.

Viva Madrid
Map E5. Calle Manuel Fernández y González 7.
Worth visiting for the decor alone, this cocktail bar bursts at the seams in summer.

SHOPPING

El Flamenco Vive
Map C5. Calle Conde de Lemos 7. Closed Sun.
This family business specializes in all things flamenco, from beautiful dresses to guitars, CDs, sheet music and DVDs.

Bureau Mad Ceramics
Map F6. Calle San Pedro 8.
Closed Mon.
This charming atelier and ceramic shop stocks antique, traditional as well as contemporary Spanish pottery.

See p80 for price codes.

BOURBON MADRID

The Bourbon monarchs expanded this area in the 18th century, building grand squares with fountains, a triumphal gateway, and what was to house a great art gallery, the Museo del Prado.

SIGHTS AT A GLANCE

Historic Buildings and Monuments
Banco de España 5
Bolsa de Comercio 7
Círculo de Bellas Artes 12
Edificio Metrópolis 14
Estación de Atocha 26
Hotel Ritz 9
Ministerio de Agricultura 23
Palacio de Comunicaciones 3
Palacio de Fernán Núñez 27
Palacio de Linares 2
Puerta de Alcalá 1
Real Academia Española 20
Real Observatorio Astronómico de Madrid 24
Teatro Español 15
Westin Palace 10

Museums and Galleries
CaixaForum 16
Casa de Lope de Vega 17
Museo del Prado 18
Museo Nacional de Antropología 25
Museo Nacional de Artes Decorativas 8
Museo Naval 6
Museo Reina Sofía (MNCARS) 28
Museo Thyssen-Bornemisza 11

Churches
Iglesia de San Jerónimo el Real 19
Iglesia de San José 13

Streets, Squares and Parks
Parque del Retiro 21
Plaza de Cibeles 4
Real Jardín Botánico 22

KEY
Metro station
Main bus stop
Railway station
Tourist information

SEE ALSO
* *Street Life p37*

◀ *The Monument of Alfonso XII in the Parque del Retiro*

View through the central arch of the Puerta de Alcalá

Puerta de Alcalá ❶

Map H4.

This ceremonial gateway is the grandest of the monuments erected by Carlos III. Finished in 1777, it marked the easternmost boundary until the mid-19th century. It now stands in the Plaza de la Independencia, and is best seen floodlit at night.

Palacio de Linares ❷

Map G4. Plaza de Cibeles 2. Exhibitions open Mon–Fri, Sat am. Free. Open for guided tours 11am, noon, 1pm Sat & Sun. Adm charge. Closed Aug.

In 1873 Amadeo I rewarded the Madrid banker José de Murga for his financial support by granting him the title of Marqués de Linares. The new aristocrat quickly set about building the most luxurious, palatial residence Madrid had ever known, resplendent in Rococo decor. The most striking rooms include the gala dining room, ballroom, the Salón China (Oriental Room) and Byzantine-style chapel. The palace was saved from 20th-century dereliction by the Spanish government's decision to restore it for Madrid's year as European Capital of Culture in 1992. The building now houses the Casa de América, an organization which promotes Latin American culture.

The height of Rococo extravagance in the Palacio de Linares ballroom

Palacio de Comunicaciones ❸

Map G4. Plaza de Cibeles. Open 10am–8pm Tue–Sun.

This impressive wedding cake of a building, built between 1905 and 1917, was once the headquarters of Spain's postal service. There is still a post office on the premises along with the headquarters of the Madrid City Council and one of the city's biggest art exhibition centres: CentroCentro. Its terrace has a fancy bar and restaurant offering charming views of the city.

Plaza de Cibeles ❹

Map G4.

In addition to being one of Madrid's best-known landmarks, the Plaza de Cibeles is also one of the most beautiful. The Fuente de Cibeles, a fine, sculpted fountain named after Cybele, the Greco-Roman goddess of nature, is con-sidered a symbol of Madrid. Four important buildings rise around the square: the Palacio de Comunicaciones; the Palacio de Linares; the army headquarters, the Cuartel General del Ejército de Tierra; and the Banco de España.

The sculpted fountain, the Fuente de Cibeles, at the Plaza de Cibeles

Banco de España is housed in this massive building

Banco de España ❺

Map F5. Calle de Alcalá. Closed to the public.

The original bank dates from 1882–91 and occupied the corner of Plaza de Cibeles. New wings were added later. The Bank of Spain itself was founded in 1856. One of the most recognizable buildings in Madrid, it was designed by the architects Sainz de la Lastra and Adano, who had studied the architecture of other European banks. The wrought-iron entrance gates, a masterpiece by the artist Bernard Asins, were opened in 1927.

Museo Naval ❻

Map G5. Paseo del Prado 5. Open 10am–7pm Tue–Sun, Aug am only. Closed on public hols. Free.

The Naval Museum has 18 display halls charting Spain's naval history. Look out for the map of the world dated 1500, showing the Americas for the first time.

Dealers in the Bolsa de Comercio, the Madrid Stock Exchange

Bolsa de Comercio 7

Map G5. Plaza de la Lealtad 1. Tel 91 709 50 00. Visits at noon Thu by appointment only. Free.

The Madrid Stock Exchange was established in 1831 and moved in 1893 to the purpose-built headquarters it currently occupies. Visitors can watch the proceedings from the Salón de los Pasos Perdidos (Hall of the Lost Steps).

Museo Nacional de Artes Decorativas 8

Map G5. Calle de Montalbán 12. Open 10am–3pm Tue–Sun (Jul & Aug am only, except Thu). Closed Mon, public hols. Adm charge. Free Thu pm, Sun am.

Housed in an aristocratic 19th-century residence, the National Museum of Decorative Arts contains an interesting collection of furniture and *objets d'art* which are mainly from Spain and date back to Phoenician times. The 18th-century kitchen is a star attraction.

Hotel Ritz 9

Map G5. Plaza de la Lealtad 5.

A few minutes' walk from the Prado *(see p34)*, this hotel is said to be Spain's most extravagant. It was commissioned in 1906, when Alfonso XIII was embarrassed by the lack of luxury accommodation in the city for his wedding guests. During the Civil War, the hotel became a hospital, and anarchist leader Buenaventura Durruti died here in 1936.

Relaxed elegance of the Palace's glass-domed Rotunda Hall lounge

Westin Palace 10

Map F5. Plaza de las Cortes 7.

The former palace of the Duque de Medinaceli was torn down to build this hotel, which opened in 1912. While its rival, the Ritz, was the exclusive reserve of its titled guests, the more informal Palace was a lively meeting place for *Madrileños*. It was the first establishment in Madrid where ladies could take tea unaccompanied. The wood-panelled Palace Bar and Rotunda Hall lounge are Madrid landmarks.

Iglesia de San Jerónimo el Real ⓳

Map G5. Calle de Moreto 4. Open daily. Free.

Built in the 16th century for Isabel I, San Jerónimo is Madrid's royal church. Alfonso XIII and Victoria Eugenia von Battenberg married here in 1906, and it is still a popular venue for society weddings.

Real Academia Española ⓴

Map G5. Calle Felipe IV 4. Closed to the public.

Spain's royal academy, founded in 1713, moved to this Neo-Classical building in 1884. The 46 members include scholars, writers and journalists. They meet regularly to assess the acceptability of any new trends in the Spanish language.

Parque del Retiro ㉑

Map H6. Park open daily. Exhibitions open 6am–10pm daily. Free.

Retiro Park, in Madrid's smart Jerónimos district, takes its name from Felipe IV's royal palace complex, which once stood here.

Iglesia de San Jerónimo el Real

Used privately by the royal family from 1632, the park became the scene of elaborate pageants, bullfights and mock naval battles. In the 18th century it was partially opened to the public, provided visitors were formally dressed, and in 1869 it was fully opened. Today, the Retiro remains one of the most popular places for relaxing in Madrid. A short stroll down the tree-lined avenue from the park's northern entrance is a pleasure lake, where rowing boats can be hired. In the Paseo de Colombia, the Casa de Vacas puts on free exhibitions of Madrid art.

Monument of Alfonso XII (1901) in the Parque del Retiro

Real Jardín Botánico ㉒

Map G6. Plaza de Murillo 2. Open daily except 25 Dec, 1 Jan.Adm charge.

South of the Prado (*see p34*) are the Royal Botanic Gardens, designed in 1781 by Gómez Ortega and Juan de Villanueva. Interest in the plants of the Philippines and South America was high in Spain at this time, and the neat beds display a large variety of medicinal plants and herbs.

Ministerio de Agricultura ㉓

Map G7. Paseo de la Infanta Isabel 1. Open noon Sat & Sun.Tel 91 468 93 60.

This magnificent, imposing late 19th-century building, originally the home of the Ministry of Development, today houses the Ministry of Agriculture. Crowning the building are allegorical sculptures. The three central figures represent Glory bestowing laurels on Science and Art.

The elaborate and daunting face of Spain's Ministerio de Agricultura

Colonnaded roof cupola of the Real Observatorio Astronómico de Madrid

Real Observatorio Astronómico de Madrid ㉔

Map H7. Calle de Alfonso XII 3. Tel 91 506 12 61. Open by appt Fri, Sat am & Sun am. Adm charge.

When it opened in 1790, Madrid's Observatorio Astronómico was one of only four observatories in Europe. There is one room open to the public where 18th- and 19th-century telescopes, as well as a Foucault pendulum, are on display. Visitors can apply in writing to peer through a telescope made in 1790 by Sir Frederick William Herschel, the astronomer who discovered Uranus.

Museo Nacional de Antropología ㉕

Map G7. Calle de Alfonso XII 68. Open 9:30am–8pm Tue–Sat, 10am–3pm Sun except some public hols. Adm charge except Sat pm, Sun.

Previously known as the Museo Nacional de Etnología, this museum was inaugurated by Alfonso XII in 1875. The ground floor houses a varied and important collection from the Philippines. The first floor is dedicated to Africa, and the second floor is the American section.

Estación de Atocha 26

Map G7. Plaza del Emperador Carlos V. Open daily.

Madrid's first rail service, from Atocha to Aranjuez, was inaugurated in 1851 by Isabel II. Forty years later, the original Atocha station was replaced by the present one. Now, it houses a palm garden. Outside, a monument commemorates the 192 people who died in the terrorist attack of 2004.

Palacio de Fernán Núñez 27

Map F6. Calle de Santa Isabel. Tel 91 151 10 02. Open by appt.

Also known as the Palacio de Cervellón, this was built for the Duke and Duchess of Fernán Núñez in 1847. It now houses the Foundation of Spanish Railways, which organizes exhibitions here. The mirrored ballroom is used for official receptions.

Museo Reina Sofía (MNCARS) 28

Map F7. Calle de Santa Isabel 52. Open Wed–Mon (times vary). Closed 1, 6 Jan, 1, 15 May, 9 Nov, 24, 25, 31 Dec & public hols. Adm charge. Free daily pm.

The highlight of this museum of 20th-century art is Picasso's Guernica (1937), but there are also major works by other influential artists, including Miró.

Jean Nouvel-designed courtyard at the Museo Reina Sofía

STREET LIFE

RESTAURANTS

La Platería
Map G6. Calle de Moratín 49. Tel 91 429 17 22.
Cheap
Situated off the Paseo del Prado, there's a terrace where you can snack on Spanish dishes, such as jamón ibérico *and goat's cheese, and delicious cakes for dessert.*

Lateral
Map E5. Plaza de Santa Ana, 12. Tel 91 420 15 82.
Moderate
Boasts an excellent location and serves a variety of tapas along with an assortment of traditional and modern delicacies.

Viridiana
Map G5. Calle Juan de Mena 14. Tel 91 531 10 39.
Expensive
Creative Spanish recipes.

BARS AND CAFÉS

Café del Círculo de Bellas Artes
Map F5. Calle del Marqués de Casa Riera 2.
Beautiful Art Deco café.

Café del Museo Thyssen-Bornemisza
Map F5. Paseo del Prado 8. Closed Mon.
A good selection of snacks, light meals and à la carte dishes.

See p80 for price codes.

AROUND LA CASTELLANA

The axis of modern Madrid is the Paseo de la Castellana, developed by the aristocracy with a string of summer palaces from Plaza de Colón northwards. To the east, the grand boulevard skirts the stylish Barrio de Salamanca. To the southwest are Chueca and Malasaña, neighbourhoods with a more authentic *Madrileño* atmosphere. The southern section of the boulevard is called the Paseo de Recoletos.

SIGHTS AT A GLANCE

Museums and Galleries

Fundación Juan March 11
Museo Arqueológico Nacional 8
Museo de Cera 6
Museo de Historia de Madrid 15
Museo Lázaro Galdiano 12
Museo del Romanticismo 14
Museo Sorolla 13

Churches

Iglesia de Santa Bárbara 4

Streets, Squares, Parks and Districts

Calle de Serrano 9
Calle del Almirante 2
Malasaña 16
Plaza de Chueca 3
Plaza de Colón 7
Salamanca 10

Historic Buildings

Café Gijón 1
Cuartel del Conde Duque 17
Palacio de Liria 18
Tribunal Supremo 5

SEE ALSO

• *Street Life p45*

KEY

Metro station
Main bus station
Tourist information

One of four enormous concrete sculptures at the *Plaza de Colón*

Interior of the literary Café Gijón

Café Gijón ❶

Map G4. Paseo de Recoletos 21. Open daily.

Madrid's café life was one of the most attractive features of the city at the turn of the 20th century. Of the many cafés that once thrived as intellectual hubs, the Gijón is one of the few to survive. It still attracts a lively literary crowd.

Calle del Almirante ❷

Map F4.

Running between the Paseo de Recoletos and Calle Barquillo, this street is famous for its dozen own-label fashion shops. For most of the 20th century it was known as "Calle de Cesterías" (basketwork street); now only one cane shop is left. The street is now referred to as "Calle de la Moda" (fashion street), and is a favourite haunt of the wealthy and local business people. However, the street also retains original shops and cafés. At No. 23 is Almirante 23, a must for browsers of antiques.

Plaza de Chueca ❸

Map F4.

Originally called Plaza de San Gregorio, this square was renamed in 1943 in honour of Federico Chueca (1846–1908), a composer of *zarzuelas* (light operas). Around the plaza is an intricate maze of little streets, an area also called Chueca. By night the area is the main focus of Madrid's gay community, with a good selection of modish bars and chic restaurants, including the trendy Mercado de San Anton that serves gourmet *tapas*.

Street cafés and apartments lining Plaza de Chueca

Iglesia de Santa Bárbara ❹

Map F3. Calle General Castaños 2. Open daily. Free.

This fine Baroque church was built, along with an adjoining convent (now the Tribunal Supremo), for Bárbara de Braganza, wife of Fernando VI. The first stone was laid in 1750 and, in 1757, the huge edifice was finished. The main door is reached through pleasant gardens, added in 1930. The extravagant interior decoration is by

Elaborately decorated interior of the Iglesia de Santa Bárbara

Doménico Olivieri. To the right of the central aisle is the tomb of Fernando VI. The tomb of Bárbara de Braganza is to the right of the altar in a separate chapel.

Tribunal Supremo 5

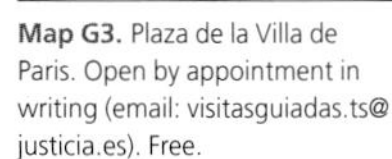

Map G3. Plaza de la Villa de Paris. Open by appointment in writing (email: visitasguiadas.ts@justicia.es). Free.

Built by François Carlier in the 1750s on the orders of Bárbara de Braganza as a convent and school for the adjoining Iglesia de Santa Bárbara, this stately Baroque building was run by the Las Salesas Reales nuns. In 1870, it became the Palace of Justice, but fell into disrepair. Restoration work was undertaken in 1991–5, and the building is now Spain's supreme court. Across the Plaza de la Villa de Paris is the Audiencía Nacional (National Court).

Museo de Cera 6

Map G3. Paseo de Recoletos 41. Open daily. Adm charge.

Madrid's wax museum houses some 450 wax dummies of famous Spanish and international figures, including Cervantes, Goya and Christopher Columbus, mostly set in scenes. Upstairs is *Multivision*, a cinema where 27 projectors are used simultaneously to show a 30-minute history of Spain.

Wax figure of Miguel de Cervantes in the Museo de Cera

Modern monument to Christopher Columbus, Plaza de Colón

museum is one of Madrid's best. It was founded by Isabel II in 1867 and contains many items uncovered during excavations all over Spain, as well as pieces from Egypt, ancient Greece and the Etruscan civilization. Highlights include Roman mosaics, coins and royal artifacts dating from the 16th–18th century. The museum also features Romanesque, Gothic and Moorish religious art.

Plaza de Colón ❼

Map G3.

This large square is dedicated to Christopher Columbus (Colón in Spanish). A pair of monuments is dedicated to the founder of the Americas. The oldest is a Neo-Gothic spire built in 1885, with Columbus at its top, pointing west. Carved reliefs on the plinth give highlights of his discoveries. Across the square is the second monument – a cluster of four large shapes inscribed with quotations relating to Columbus' historic journey to America.

Museo Arqueológico Nacional ❽

Map G4. Calle de Serrano 13. Open Tue–Sun except 1, 6 Jan, 1 May, 24, 25, 31 Dec. Free.

With hundreds of exhibits, ranging from prehistoric times to the 19th century, this renovated palatial

Calle de Serrano ❾

Map H3.

Named after a 19th-century politician, Madrid's smartest shopping street runs north from the Plaza de la Independencia to the Plaza del Ecuador, in the district of Salamanca. Several top Spanish designers, including Adolfo Domínguez and Roberto Verino, have boutiques in the middle of the street, and Hermès, Valentino and Chanel have shops on the nearby Calle de José Ortega y Gasset.

Salamanca ❿

Map H2.

Madrid's Barrio de Salamanca (Salamanca district) was developed in 1862–3 as an area for the bourgeoisie, and takes its name from its founder, José "Pepito" Salamanca, Marqués de Salamanca (1811–83). He inaugurated his superb palace at Paseo de Recoletos 10, now the BBVA

Statue of Columbus, Plaza de Colón

Statue of Salamanca's founder, the Marqués de Salamanca

Fund (Banco Bilbao Vizcaya Argentaria) in 1858, and by 1862 had begun developing the land behind it. He also built the first tramways in Madrid, connecting the Barrio de Salamanca with the centre of Madrid. Some of Madrid's best shops can be found here, as well as some discreet restaurants.

Fundación Juan March ⓫

Map J2. Calle de Castelló 77. Open 11am–8pm Mon–Fri, 11am–2pm Sat, public hols. Free.

Established in 1955 with an endowment from financier Juan March, this cultural and scientific foundation is best known for its art exhibitions and concerts. Works by Kandinsky, Picasso and Matisse have been shown here, alongside a permanent collection of over 1,300 contemporary Spanish pieces. The second-floor library has a collection of contemporary Spanish music, with listening desks, and there is also a library of contemporary Spanish theatre. A 400-seat auditorium hosts free concerts.

Museo Lázaro Galdiano ⓬

Map H1. Calle Serrano 122. Open daily except Tue, public hols. Adm charge. Free 3:30–4:30pm, 2–3pm Sun.

This Neo-Renaissance mansion houses nearly 3,000 items from the private collection of financier and editor José Lázaro Galdiano (1862–1947). The exhibits, ranging from the 7th century BC to the 20th century, include archaeological finds, religious artifacts, Limoges enamels, Old Masters, paintings by non-Spanish artists, medieval ivory, armour, jewellery and silver.

Sculpture by Berrocol, by the main entrance to the Fundación Juan March

Former studio of Impressionist Joaquín Sorolla, Museo Sorolla

Museo Sorolla ⓭

Map G1. Paseo del General Martínez Campos 37. Open daily except Mon, public hols. Adm charge. Free Sat pm & Sun am.

The studio-mansion of Valencian Impressionist painter Joaquín Sorolla, who died in 1923, is now a museum exhibiting his art. Also on display here are various objects collected during the artist's lifetime, including tiles and ceramics.

Museo del Romanticismo ⓮

Map E3. Calle de San Mateo 13. Open Tue–Sat, Sun am. Closed 1, 6 Jan, 1 May, 24, 25, 31 Dec. Adm charge. Free Sat pm & Sun.

This is a small Neo-Classical mansion with a charming garden, designed in 1776. By 1924, Marqués de la Vega-Inclán,had turned it into a museum and donated 19th-century paintings, books and furniture. In 1927 the museum was acquired by the state, and reorganized to look like the home of a wealthy mid-19th-century family, evoking the Romantic period. The exhibits are housed on the first floor of the building. The Mariano José de Larra Room is dedicated to this great satirical journalist and writer. Among his personal effects is the duelling pistol he used to kill himself, after being rejected by his lover.

Museo de Historia de Madrid ⓯

Map E3. Calle de Fuencarral 78. Tel 91 701 18 63. Open 9:30am–7pm Tue–Sun. Free.

In the former hospice of St Ferdinand with its superb Baroque façade, the museum was inaugurated in 1929. The basement is devoted to the city's archaeology, while upstairs are maps showing how radically Madrid has been transformed. Among them is Pedro Texeiro's 1656 map, thought to be the oldest of the city. There is also a meticulous model of Madrid made in 1830.

Baroque façade by Pedro de Ribera, Museo de Historia de Madrid

Malasaña ⓰

Map D3.

Officially called Barrio de Maravillas (District of Miracles) after a 17th-century church that once stood here, this bohemian area is more widely known as Malasaña. The charming cobbled

The main altar of Iglesia de San Plácido in Malasaña

streets boast pretty fountains and plenty of trees. At night the streets are thronged with people looking for a wild time. Malasaña is also rich in sites of historical interest.

Cuartel del Conde Duque ⓱

Map C3. Calle del Conde Duque 11. Open Tue–Sat, Sun am. Free.

This enormous complex houses a police station, council offices, a library, a cultural centre and the Museo Municipal de Arte Contemporáneo.

Palacio de Liria ⓲

Map C3. Calle de la Princesa 20. Open by appointment Fri am. Closed mid-Jun–Sep, mid-Dec–mid-Jan.

This lavish building was the residence of the Alba family, and is still owned by the Duke. It houses the Albas' outstanding collection of art including work by Titian, Rubens and Rembrandt, and Goya's 1795 portrait of the then Duchess of Alba.

STREET LIFE

RESTAURANTS

La Dominga
Map D3. Calle del Espíritu Santo 15. Tel 91 523 38 09.
Cheap
Casual restaurant with a pleasant ambience offering Mediterranean cuisine.

Media Ración
Map F3. Calle de la Beneficencia 15. Tel 91 447 51 11.
Moderate
Fernando Cuenllas' new, elegant restaurant, also serves half portion dishes.

La Manduca de Azagra
Map E2. Calle de Sagasta 14 Tel 91 591 01 12.
Expensive
This restaurant with minimalist decor serves seasonal cuisine.

BARS AND CAFÉS

La Ardosa
Map E3. Calle de Colón 13. Tel 91 521 49 79.
This cosy taberna's best-known customer was the painter Francisco de Goya. Excellent, imaginative tapas.

El Comunista
Map E4. Calle de Augusto Figueroa 35. Tel 91 521 70 12.
Authentic taberna offering simple home cooking.

SHOPPING

Salvador Bachiller
Map H3. Calle de Velázquez 24.
A stunning boutique offering leather goods as well as house accessories.

See p80 for price codes.

FURTHER AFIELD

Several of Madrid's best sights lie outside the city centre. Museums describe the development of the city and display artifacts from Spain's former colonies. Other historic buildings range from the Egyptian Templo de Debod to the old-style apartment building of La Corrala. To the north lies the commercial district of Azca, and west, across the Río Manzanares, is Madrid's vast, green recreation ground, the Casa de Campo.

SIGHTS AT A GLANCE

Historic Buildings
Estación de Príncipe Pío 16
La Corrala 11
Puente de Segovia and Río Manzanares 13
Puerta de Toledo 12
Real Fábrica de Tapices 9
Sala del Canal de Isabel II 3
Templo de Debod 15

Churches and Convents
Ermita de San Antonio de la Florida 14

Museums and Galleries
Matadero Madrid 8
Museo Casa de la Moneda 7
Museo de América 1
Museo de Ciencias Naturales 5
Museo del Traje 2
Museo del Ferrocarril 10

Squares, Parks and Districts
Azca 4
Plaza de Toros de Las Ventas 6

0 km 2
0 miles 2

KEY
Railway station

Sights Outside the Centre

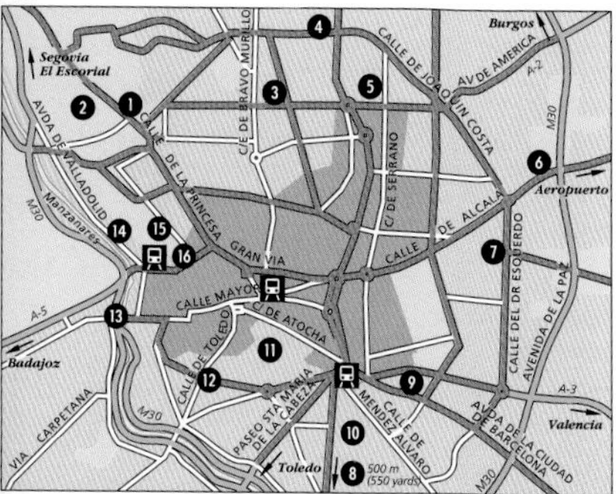

Mudéjar arches and tilework on the Plaza de Toros de Las Ventas

Museo de América ❶

Avenida de los Reyes Católicos 6. Open Tue–Sun except some public hols. Adm charge. Free Sun.

A unique collection of artifacts relating to Spain's colonization of the Americas is housed here. Highlights include the rare Mayan *Códice Tro-cortesiano* (AD 1250–1500) from Mexico and pre-Columbian gold and silver objects from around AD 500–1000.

The Mirador del Faro alongside the Museo de América

Museo del Traje ❷

Avenida Juan de Herrera 2. Open Tue–Sun. Closed 1, 6 Jan, 1 May, 9 Nov, 24, 25, 31 Dec. Adm charge. Free Sat pm & Sun.

This museum showcases the style of garments over the years from traditional 16th-century outfits to Spanish designer wear from the 20th century.

Sala del Canal de Isabel II ❸

Calle de Santa Engracia 125. Open Tue–Sat, Sun am & public hols am. Closed 1 Jan, 25 Dec. Free.

This water tower is used as a venue for photographic

Sala del Canal de Isabel II

exhibitions but most visitors come to marvel at its complex construction. Built between 1908 and 1911, it is 36 m (118 ft) high, surmounted by a vast water tank. Out of service since the mid-20th century, it is now a stylish exhibition space.

Azca ❹

This "mini-Manhattan" stretches from the Nuevos Ministerios complex to the Palacio de Congresos y Exposiciones. Across from the Plaza de Lima is the Estadio Santiago Bernabéu, home of Real Madrid Football Club. Among the tower blocks, hotels, cinemas, restaurants and bars are the Plaza Pablo Ruiz Picasso, and the Torre Picasso, the office building by World Trade Center architect Minoru Yamasaki.

Museo de Ciencias Naturales ❺

Calle José Gutierrez Abascal 2. Open Tue–Sun. Closed 1, 6 Jan, 1 May, 25 Dec. Adm charge.

This natural history museum contains 16,400 minerals,

220 meteorites, 30,000 birds and mammals and many more items in its archives. An interactive computer display provides insights into the sounds and habitats of animals. There is also a cross-section of the Atapuerca site, where Europe's earliest human remains (c. 780,000 years old) were found in 1997.

Plaza de Toros de Las Ventas ❻

Calle de Alcalá 237.
Open for bullfights, concerts and guided visits. Tel 687 739 032. Museo Taurino open 10am–5:30pm daily.

Built in 1929 in Neo-Mudéjar style, Las Ventas replaced the city's original bullring, which stood near the Puerta de Alcalá *(see p28)*. In September and October the bullring is used as a rock concert venue. The Museo Taurino features bullfighting photos and memorabilia.

Museo Casa de la Moneda ❼

Calle del Doctor Esquerdo 36.
Open Tue–Fri, Sat & Sun (am only) except public hols. Free.

The Spanish Mint and stamp factory is located in a vast granite building, which includes the renovated museum. Here you can trace the history of currency, from salt to the euro.

Matadero Madrid ❽

Plaza de Legazpi 8.
Open 9am–10pm daily. Free.

A former slaughterhouse in the Arganzuela district, Matadero Madrid was converted into a contemporary arts centre in 2005. This gorgeous structure was originally envisioned as a complex of pavilions. The architecture incorporates Neo-Mudéjar features such as tiles with abstract designs. Matadero also has three spaces where visitors can enjoy a meal or a drink or simply relax.

Plaza de Toros de Las Ventas, Madrid's beautiful Neo-Mudéjar bullring

Real Fábrica de Tapices 9

Calle de Fuenterrabía 2. Open for guided visits only Mon–Fri (10am–2pm) except public hols, Aug. Adm charge.

The Royal Tapestry Factory is the only one which has survived of those opened by the Bourbons in the 18th century. Visitors can see the making by hand of the carpets and tapestries, a process that has changed little since the factory was built.

Cafeteria of the Museo del Ferrocarril, set in a 1930s dining car

Museo del Ferrocarril 10

Paseo de las Delicias 61. Open Mon–Sun 10am–3pm except 1, 6 Jan, 1 May, 15–30 Aug, 25 Dec. Adm charge.

In 1880 Madrid's first railway terminus opened – Delicias Station. It remained in use until 1971, then re-opened in 1984 as a museum. On display are more than 30 locomotives – steam, diesel and electric – as well as rolling stock. You can explore some of the carriages, including a 1930s dining car that is now the cafeteria.

La Corrala 11

Calle de Mesón de Paredes. Closed to the public.

Corralas are timber-framed apartment blocks, built in 19th century to house the poor. La Corrala (1872) exemplifies this type of housing. In 1977, it was declared a monument of historic interest, and restored. On summer nights, it is used as a backdrop for outdoor light opera.

Puerta de Toledo 12

Glorieta de Puerta de Toledo.

This triumphal arch was commissioned in 1813 by Joseph Bonaparte, José I. One of Madrid's two remaining city gates, it is topped by a group of sculptures that represent a personification of Spain.

Puente de Segovia and Río Manzanares 13

Calle de Segovia.

Puente de Segovia, which spans Río Manzanares, was commissioned by Felipe II. Work began in 1582, and the bridge was rebuilt in 1682.

The buttressed arches of Puente de Segovia over the Río Manzanares

Ermita de San Antonio de la Florida 14

Glorieta San Antonio de la Florida. Open daily except Mon, public hols. Free.

Goya enthusiasts should not miss this remarkable Neo-Classical church, built during the reign of Carlos IV. Goya painted the cupola's fine fresco of St Anthony in 1798, and the artist lies buried under the dome of the church.

Templo de Debod 15

Calle Ferraz 1. Open Tue–Fri, Sat & Sun except public hols. Free.

The authentic Egyptian Temple of Debod, built in the 2nd century BC, was given to Spain in 1968 by the Egyptian government. The temple's carvings depict Amen, a ram-headed Theban god symbolizing life and fertility, to whom the temple is dedicated. It is worth visiting the temple in the evening to see it beautifully illuminated.

The remodelled Estacion del Norte station and shopping center

Estación de Príncipe Pío 16

Paseo de la Florida. Shopping centre open Mon–Sat 10am–10pm, Sun 11am–10pm. Restaurants open until 2am.

Also known as Estación del Norte, this railway station was opened in 1880 to supply train services between Madrid and the north of Spain. In 1915, the station's look was enhanced by Mudéjar-style pavilions designed by Demetrio Ribes. The entrance façade was added by architect Luis Martínez Ribes in 1926. Located in the main building is a commercial centre with cinemas, restaurants and numerous shops. Another part of the station is a major transport interchange.

Egyptian temple of Debod, with two of its original gateways

BEYOND MADRID

Spain's central plateau consists mainly of wheat fields and plains. Yet it also has mountains, gorges, forests and lakes filled with wildlife, while the towns and cities are permeated with history, reflected in some stunning architecture – Toledo's Gothic cathedral, Segovia's alcázar and the 15th-century castle at Manzanares el Real.

SIGHTS AT A GLANCE

Alcalá de Henares 12
Buitrago del Lozoya 8
Chinchón 15
El Escorial pp54–7 1
Guadalajara 11
Illescas 17
La Granja de San Ildefonso 6
Manzanares el Real 3
Monasterio de Santa María de El Paular 5
Museo del Aire 14
Palacio de El Pardo 13
Palacio Real de Aranjuez 16
Santa Cruz del Valle de los Caídos 2
Segovia pp62–65 7
Sierra Centro de Guadarrama 4
Sierra Norte 9
Sigüenza 10
Toledo pp70–73 18

0 km 40
0 miles 40

KEY

International Airport

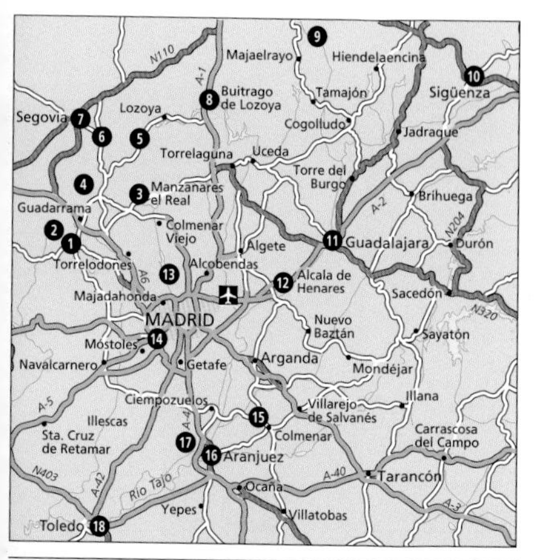

◄ *Exterior of Museo del Greco in Toledo*

El Escorial ❶

Set in the foothills northwest of Madrid, Felipe II's imposing grey palace of San Lorenzo de El Escorial was built between 1563 and 1584, and its unornamented severity set a new architectural style. Its artistic wealth includes some of the most important works of art of the royal Habsburg collections.

The Royal Pantheon *contains the funerary urns of Spanish monarchs*

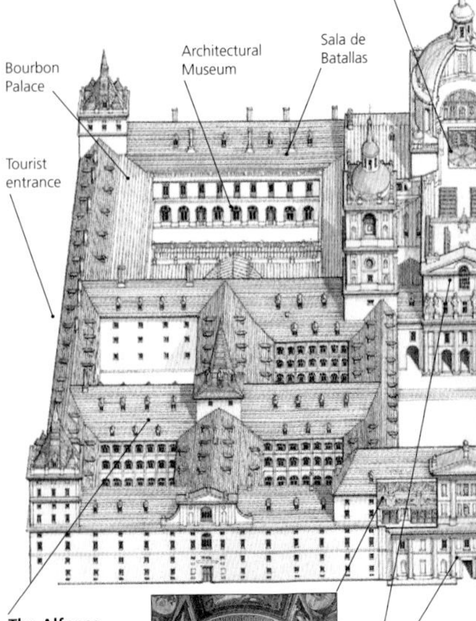

The Alfonso XII College *was founded in 1875 as a boarding school.*

The Library *held Felipe II's personal collection of books.*

The Basílica *is a huge, decorated church with a lavish altarpiece.*

The plain architectural style of El Escorial is called desornamentado, *literally "unadorned"*

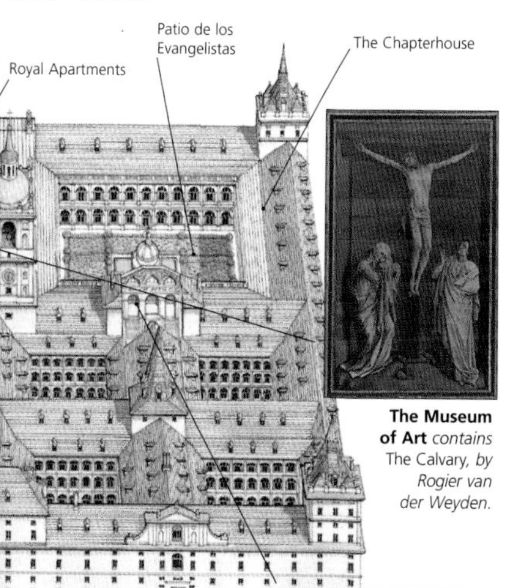

The Museum of Art *contains* The Calvary, *by Rogier van der Weyden.*

The Glory of the Spanish Monarchy *by Luca Giordano depicts Carlos I, Felipe II and the building of the monastery.*

VISITORS' CHECKLIST

Paseo de Juan de Borbón y Batemberg. Open 10am–8pm Tue–Sun (until 6pm Oct–Mar). Closed public hols. Adm charge. Free Wed & Thu pm (times vary) for EU residents. **www.patrimonionacional.es**

Exploring El Escorial

Felipe II built this palace as the final resting place of his revered father, Carlos I of Spain – Holy Roman Emperor Charles V – whom he succeeded in 1556. Felipe II, as King of Naples, Sicily, Milan, The Netherlands, Spain and the New World, used the finest talent available to decorate the austere monastery. The official tour goes through the Royal Apartments and Royal Pantheon in 45 minutes, leaving you to explore the rest by yourself.

Royal Apartments

The Palacio de los Austrias, or Royal Apartments, are built around and adjoining the basilica. The Sala de Retratos is full of portraits, beginning above the fireplace with *Carlos I* by Juan Pantoja de la Cruz (1553–1608) – a copy of the original painting by Titian lost in a fire in 1604. At both ends of the Salas de los Paseos are magnificent German marquetry doors.

Pantheons

Directly beneath the high altar of the basilica is the Royal Pantheon, where almost all Spanish monarchs since Carlos *0* are laid to rest. Kings lie on the left of the altar and queens on the right. The most recent addition to the pantheon is the mother of Juan Carlos I.

Chapterhouses

The Salas Capitulares, or Chapterhouses contain wooden benches for the monastery's 100 monks. These four light and spacious rooms with their fine vaulted ceilings are decorated with numerous allegorical paintings.
The enamelled, gold-plated wooden retable of Carlos I, Holy Roman Emperor Charles V, can be seen here. The king took this portable altar with him on military campaigns.

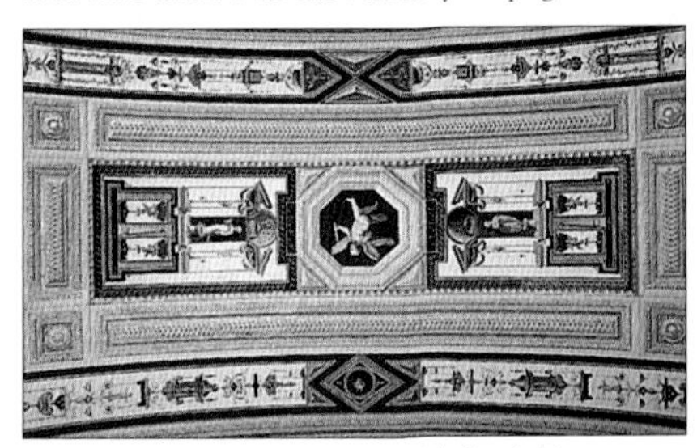

The Chapterhouse ceilings are decorated with allegorical frescoes

Fresco by Luca Giordano

The Museums

Within El Escorial there are several small museums. The north façade entrance leads to St Maurice's Hall. Nearby stairs lead down to the small Architectural Museum which contains plans, models and engravings of the palace. Upstairs, the Museum of Art contains mainly works from the 16th and 17th centuries. The long fourth room is dominated by the superb *Calvary* by Rogier van der Weyden (c. 1400–64).

The Library

Established by Felipe II, this was the first public library in Spain, and boasts a vaulted ceiling and a mar-ble floor. In 1619 the king issued a decree that a copy of each new publication in his empire should be sent to him. At its zenith, it contained some 40,000 books and manuscripts, mainly from the 15th and 16th centuries.

The Basílica

Historically, only the aristocracy entered the basilica; townspeople were confined to the vestibule at the entrance. The basilica contains 45 altars. Among its highlights are the exquisite marble of *Christ Crucified* (1562) by Benvenuto Cellini. Either side of the altar, above doors leading to the royal bedrooms in the Palacio de los Austrias, are gilded bronze cenotaphs of Carlos I and Felipe II worshipping with their families. The enormous altarpiece was designed by Juan de Herrera.

Decorated altarpiece, Basílica

Palace of the Bourbons

In contrast to the simple rooms of the Palacio de los Austrias (Felipe II's royal apartments), the Bourbon apartments are sumptuous. They were created by Carlos IV, and are hung with framed tapestries, some by Goya, from the Real Fábrica de Tapices (*see p50*).

The gigantic memorial cross at Valle de los Caídos

Santa Cruz del Valle de los Caídos ❷

North of El Escorial on M600. Only the basilica is open: 10am–7pm Tue–Sun (6:30pm in summer). Tel 91 890 54 11. Adm charge. Free Wed & Thu from 4pm.

General Franco (1892–1975) had the Holy Cross of the Valley of the Fallen built as a memorial to those who died in the Spanish Civil War (1936–9). The vast cross is located some 13 km (8 miles) north of El Escorial *(see pp54–7)*, and can be seen for miles in every direction. Some Spaniards find it too chilling a symbol of the dictatorship to be enjoyable, while for others its sheer size is rewarding. The cross is 150 m (490 ft) high and rises above a basilica carved 250 m (820 ft) deep into the rock by prisoners of war. A number of them are said to have died during the 20-year project. Next to the basilica's high altar is the plain white tombstone of Franco himself and, opposite, that of José Antonio Primo de Rivera, founder of the fascist Falange Española party. Another 40,000 coffins of soldiers who fought on both sides in the war lie here out of sight, including those of two unidentified victims.

Manzanares el Real ❸

M607 to Colmenar Viejo & M608. Market: Tue, Fri. Festivals: Fiesta de Verano (early Aug), Cristo de la Nave (14 Sep).

The skyline of Manzanares el Real is dominated by its restored 15th-century castle. Although equipped with some traditional military features, the castle was used mainly as a residential palace by the Dukes of Infantado. Below the castle is a 16th-century church, a Renaissance portico and fine capitals. Behind the town, bordering the foothills of the Sierra de Guadarrama, is La Pedriza, a mass of granite screes and ravines very popular with climbers. It is now part of a nature reserve.

Sierra Centro de Guadarrama ❹

The central section of the Sierra de Guadarrama was linked to Madrid by train in

Enthralling Navacerrada mountain pass

the 1920s. The pine-covered granite slopes are now dotted with holiday chalets. Villages such as Navacerrada and Cercedilla have grown into popular resorts for ski-ing, mountain biking, rock climbing, horse riding and walking. The a, a nature reserve of wild forests, is best reached via Cercedilla. It has a well-preserved stretch of Roman road, as well as picnic spots and marked walks.

Monasterio de Santa María de El Paular ❺

Southwest of Rascafría on M604. Open 11am–1:30pm, 4–6:30pm daily. Closed Thu. Adm charge.

Castile's first Carthusian monastery was founded in 1390 on the site of a medieval royal hunting lodge. Although this monastery was built in the Gothic style, many Plateresque and Renaissance features were added later. In the 1950s the state restored it, and today the complex comprises a private hotel, a working Benedictine monastery and a church. The monastery constitutes an excellent starting point from which to explore the country towns of Rascafría and Lozoya in the surrounding Lozoya valley. To the southwest lies the Lagunas de Peñalara nature reserve.

Altarpiece in the Monasterio de Santa María de El Paular

Serenely beautiful royal gardens at La Granja de San Ildefonso

La Granja de San Ildefonso ❻

Plaza de España 15, Segovia. Open Tue–Sun. Gardens open daily. Palace & gardens closed 1, 6, 23 Jan, 1 May, 25 Aug, 24, 25, 31 Dec. Adm charge. Free Wed & Thu afternoons for EU residents.

This pleasure palace, on the site of a hunting lodge, was begun by Felipe V in 1720. There are countless decorated salons, the church is adorned in high Baroque style and the Royal Mausoleum contains the tomb of Felipe V and his queen, Isabel de Farnesio. The garden fountains portray Felipe V and his queen as Apollo and Diana. They run on Wednesdays and Saturdays at 5:30pm and Sundays at 1pm.

Segovia ❼

See pp62–5.

Buitrago del Lozoya ❽

Madrid. Market: Sat. Festivals: La Asunción y San Roque (15 Aug), Cristo de los Esclavos (15 Sep). Museo Picasso open daily except Mon, Sun pm. Free.

Picturesquely sited above a meander in the Río Lozoya is the town of Buitrago del Lozoya. Founded by the Romans and fortified by the Arabs, it became a bustling medieval market town. The ruined 14th-century Gothic-Mudéjar castle is used as a venue for bullfights and a festival of theatre and music in the summer. The old

Buitrago del Lozoya, standing next to the river

quarter, within the town's walls, retains its charming atmosphere. In the basement of the town hall on the Plaza de Picasso is the small Museo Picasso.

Sierra Norte ❾

The black slate hamlets of the Sierra Norte, which was once known as the Sierra Pobre (Poor Sierra), are located in the most rural part of Madrid province. At Montejo de la Sierra, the largest village in the area, an information centre organizes riding, rental of traditional houses and visits to the nature reserve of the Hayedo de Montejo de la Sierra. From Montejo, you can drive to hamlets such as La Hiruela or Puebla de la Sierra. The drier southern hills slope down to the Embalse de Puentes Viejas, a reservoir where summer chalets cluster around artificial beaches. On the eastern edge of the Sierra Norte lies Patones, which escaped invasion by the Moors and Napoleon due to its location.

Sigüenza ❿

Guadalajara. Market: Sat. Festivals: San Juan (24 Jun), San Roque (15 Aug).

Dominating the hillside town of Sigüenza is its impressive castle-parador. The Romanesque cathedral in the old town was begun in the 12th century. In one of the chapels is the Tomb of El Doncel (the young nobleman), built for Martín

Figure of El Doncel on his tomb in Sigüenza cathedral

Vázquez de Arce, Isabel of Castile's pageboy who was killed in a battle against the Moors in 1486.

Guadalajara ⓫

Market: Tue, Sat. Festivals: Virgen de la Antigua (Sep). Palacio de los Duques del Infantado: museum closed Mon, Sun pm, public hols. Palace open daily. Free.

Traces of Guadalajara's past splendour survive. The Palacio de los Duques del Infantado (now the Museo Provincial), built from the 14th to the 17th century, is an outstanding example of Gothic-Mudéjar architecture.

Stonework on the façade of the Palacio de los Duques del Infantado

Segovia 7

Segovia is the most spectacularly sited city in Spain. The old town is set high on a rocky spur surrounded by the Río Eresma and Río Clamores. A relatively short journey from Madrid, Segovia is readily accessible, easy to negotiate on foot, and there is plenty to see and do for a day trip or an overnight stay. The view of the old town from the valley below at sunset is magical.

Tower of San Esteban

① Cathedral

Plaza Mayor. Open daily. Adm charge. Free Sun am.

Dating from 1525, this massive Gothic structure replaced the old cathedral, which was destroyed in 1520. The old cloister survived and was rebuilt on the new site. Architect Juan Gil de Hontañón devised the austere but elegant design. The pinnacles, flying buttresses, tower and dome form an impressive silhouette. The interior is light and elegantly vaulted, with stained-glass windows. It has a high altar designed by Francisco Sabatini in 1768. More than 20 beautiful chapels, most enclosed by graceful ironwork grilles, line the nave and apse. The most interesting is the Chapel of the Pietà, which took its name from the beautiful sculpture by Juan de Juni. The cloister, whose pointed arches are divided by slender mullions and perforated tracery, is accessed through an outstanding Gothic arch by Juan Guas in the Chapel of Christ's Solace. The cloister leads to the chapterhouse museum, which houses 17th-century Brussels tapestries, paintings, sculptures, silverware, furniture, books and coins.

② Museo de Segovia

Casa del Sol, Calle Socorro 11. Open Tue–Sat, Sun am. Closed 1, 6 Jan, 24, 25, 31 Dec, public hols. Adm charge. Free Sat & Sun.

This archaeological museum contains 15,000-year-old Stone Age engravings as well as tools, arms, pottery and metalwork through the

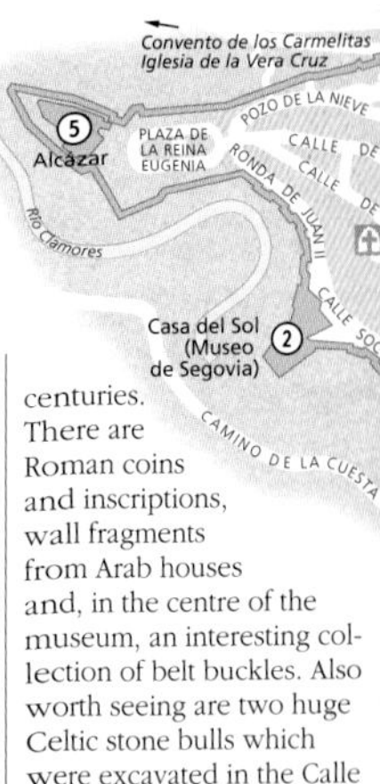

centuries. There are Roman coins and inscriptions, wall fragments from Arab houses and, in the centre of the museum, an interesting collection of belt buckles. Also worth seeing are two huge Celtic stone bulls which were excavated in the Calle

The Alcázar, like a fairy-tale castle rising above the cliff (see p64)

Mayor. It is thought the bulls may have been divine protectors of people or livestock. In the nearby province of Avila, such icons are linked with burials.

SEGOVIA CITY CENTRE

Cathedral ①
Museo de Segovia ②
Casa de los Picos ③
Aqueduct ④
Alcázar ⑤
Palacio Episcopal ⑥

KEY

P Parking
Tourist information
Church
Convent or monastery

The 15th-century Casa de los Picos

③ Casa de los Picos

Calle Juan Bravo 8. Open daily.

Just inside the city walls is the Casa de los Picos, a mansion whose 15th-century façade is adorned with diamond-shaped stones. It houses an art gallery and school.

④ Aqueduct

In use until the late 19th century, this aqueduct was built at the end of the 1st century AD by the Romans, who turned ancient Segovia into a military base. With this feat of engineering, water from the Río Frío flowed into the city, filtered through tanks on the way.

⑤ Alcázar

Plaza de la Reina Victoria Eugenia. Open daily except public hols. Adm charge.

Although there has been a fortress on this site since the Middle Ages, the present castle is mostly a reconstruction following a fire in 1862. Its rooms are decorated with armour, paintings and furniture for a medieval atmosphere. There is also a weaponry museum. The castle had its heyday in the Middle Ages. The rectangular Juan II tower was completed during the reign of Enrique IV in the 15th century. It is worth climbing to the top for breathtaking views of Segovia and the Guadarrama mountains.

⑥ Palacio Episcopal

Plaza de San Esteban. Open 10am–2pm, 4:30–7pm daily.

Built for the Salcedos family, this 16th-century building was later acquired by Bishop Murillo. Its museum is now closed to the public.

The Roman aqueduct running through the old town

VISITORS' CHECKLIST

Tourist information: Plaza Azoguejo 1. Tel 921 466 67 20. Market: Tue, Thu, Sat. Festivals: San Juan (24 Jun), San Pedro (29 Jun), San Frutos (25 Oct). **www.turismodesegovia.com**

Monasterio de El Parral

Calle del Parral 2. Open Wed–Sun. Donation.

Just north of the city walls, this monastery has four cloisters and a Plateresque altarpiece. It contains the Plateresque tombs of its benefactor, the Marqués de Villena, and his wife, María.

Monasterio de los Carmelitas

Alameda de la Fuencisla. Open daily. Donation.

In a secluded Eresma valley, St John of the Cross founded this convent in the 16th century and was Prior until 1591.

Segovia's Churches

Segovia is dotted with many notable churches, including the 11th-century Romanesque **San Juan de los Caballeros**, with a fine sculptured portico; 13th-century **San Esteban** with a five-storey tower; and 11th-century **San Martín** with its arcades, capitals and gilded altarpiece. The **Iglesia de San Millán**, a Romanesque jewel in the newer part of town, has a Mozarabic tower and a 14th-century Gothic crucifix. The **Iglesia de la Vera Cruz**, outside the old town, is a 12-sided crusader's church (1208).

The tree-lined Plaza Mayor

STREET LIFE

RESTAURANTS

El Bernardino
Calle Cervantes 2.
Tel 92 146 24 77.
Moderate
Traditional Segovian cooking is served in this popular restaurant. Fixed-price menu.

Mesón de Cándido
Plaza del Azoguejo 5.
Tel 92 142 59 11.
Expensive
Don't leave town without visiting Mesón de Cándido. The restaurant has good views of the Roman aqueduct and serves local specialities such as roast lamb and suckling pig.

BARS

Bar José María
Calle Cronista Lecea 11.
Tel 92 146 11 11.
Moderately priced tapas *in the bar-annexe to the excellent Restaurant José Maria.*

La Tasquina
Calle Valdeláguila 3.
Tel 92 146 39 14.
Friendly bar with an excellent collection of wines accompanied by delicious tapas.

See p80 for price codes.

Façade of Colegio de San Ildefonso in Alcalá de Henares

Alcalá de Henares ⓬

Madrid. Market: Mon, Wed. Festivals: Feria de Alcalá (late Aug). Casa-Museo de Cervantes: open daily except Mon, public hols. Free. Palacete Laredo: open Sat & Sun (except Aug). Adm charge.

At the heart of Alcalá is one of Spain's most renowned university quarters. Founded in 1499, Alcalá's university became one of the foremost places of learning in 16th-century Europe, although most of the original colleges are now gone. The Casa-Museo de Cervantes was once the home of Miguel de Cervantes (1547–1616) who was born in Alcalá.

Palacio de El Pardo ⓭

Northwest of Madrid on A6. Open daily except during royal visits, public hols. Adm charge. Free Wed & Thu afternoons for EU residents.

This royal hunting lodge and palace, set in parkland, includes General Franco among its former residents. A tour takes visitors around the palace's original Habsburg wing and 18th-century extension. The Bourbon interior is decorated with frescoes, gilt mouldings and tapestries. The palace is used to entertain heads of state and royalty.

Museo del Aire ⓮

Cuatro Vientos airfield. Open 10am–2pm Tue–Sun. Closed 1, 6 Jan, Easter, Aug, 12 Oct, 10, 24, 25, 31 Dec. Free.

The star exhibit at the museum of Spanish aviation is the Breguet-XIX *Jesús del Gran Poder*, which made the first Spanish transatlantic flight in 1929. Others include the 1911 Vilanova-Acedo, one of the first planes made in Spain. Prototypes of various Spanish aircraft include the Saeta, Super Saeta and the Casa C–101 Aviojet. The museum also charts the lives of famous aviators.

Early Lufthansa aircraft at the Museo del Aire

Chinchón ⓯

Madrid. Market: Sat. Festivals: Semana Santa (Easter Week), San Roque (12–18 Aug).

Chinchón is Madrid province's most picturesque town. The 16th-century, typically Castilian, porticoed Plaza Mayor comes alive

Chinchón's unique porticoed Plaza Mayor, occasionally used for bullfights

for the Easter passion play and during the August bullfights. *Madrileños* often come to the town at weekends to sample the superb *chorizo* and locally produced anís in the town's many taverns.

Palacio Real de Aranjuez 16

Plaza de Parejas, Aranjuez. Open daily except Mon. Gardens open daily. Closed 1, 6 Jan, 1 May, 24, 25, 31 Dec. Adm charge. Free Wed & Thu afternoons for EU residents.

The royal summer palace and gardens of Aranjuez grew up around a medieval hunting lodge standing beside a natural weir, the meeting point of the Tagus and Jarama rivers. Visit Aranjuez for the pleasure of walking in shady royal gardens which inspired Joaquín Rodrigo's famous musical composition *Concierto de Aranjuez*. At the far end of the garden stands the Casa del Labrador (Labourer's Cottage), a richly decorated pavilion built by Carlos IV. In summer, a 19th-century steam train, built to take strawberries to the market in Madrid, runs between Aranjuez and the capital.

The Palacio Real de Aranjuez set next to the Tigus and Jarama rivers

Illescas 17

Toledo. Market: Thu. Festivals: Fiesta de Milagro (11 Mar), Fiesta Patronal (31 Aug). Hospital de Nuestra Señora de la Caridad: open Mon–Sat. Adm charge.

The town of Illescas was the summer venue for the court of Felipe II. There is little to see in the old town, but it has two interesting churches: the Parroquial de la Asunción, built between the 13th and 16th centuries, and easily identified by its Mudéjar tower; and the 16th-century church of the Hospital de Nuestra Señora de la Caridad, which boasts an important art collection.

The picturesque Monasterio de El Parral in Segovia ▶

Toledo ⓲

Toledo is easily reached from Madrid by rail, bus or car, and is then best explored on foot. To visit all the main sights you need at least two days, but it is possible to walk around the medieval and Jewish quarters on a long morning.

Alcázar

Calle Unión s/n.
Army museum: open 11am–5pm Thu–Tue.
Adm charge. Library: open Mon–Fri, Sat am.

The fortified palace of Carlos I (Holy Roman Emperor Charles V) stands on the site of former Roman, Visigothic and Muslim fortresses. The building now houses an army museum. The Alcázar library contains many early books and maunuscripts.

Carlos V triumphant over a Moor

Museo de Santa Cruz

Calle Miguel de Cervantes 3.
Open daily. Closed Sun pm. Free.

This museum's collection is focuses on medieval and Renaissance works of art. There are also paintings by El Greco, including one of his last, *The Assumption* (1613). Displays include Toledan armour, damascened swords, ceramics and Roman archaeological artifacts.

Iglesia de Santo Tomé

Plaza del Conde. Open daily.
Adm charge.

Visitors come to Santo Tomé mainly to admire El Greco's masterpiece, *The Burial of the Count of Orgaz*. The painting has never been moved. The church is thought to be from the 12th century, and its tower is one of the best examples of Mudéjar architecture in the city.

Sinagoga del Tránsito

Calle Samuel Leví.
Open Tue–Sat, Sun am except 1, 6 Jan, 1 May, 10 Jun, 24, 25, 31 Dec. Adm charge.
Free Sat pm, Sun am.

The most elaborate Mudéjar interior in the city is hidden behind the humble façade of this former 13th-century synagogue. Adjoining the synagogue is a museum of Spanish Jewish culture.

Iglesia de Santo Tomé

Sinagoga de Santa María la Blanca

Calle de los Reyes Católicos 4. Open daily. Closed 1 Jan, 25 Dec. Adm charge.

The oldest and largest of the city's eight original synagogues, this monument dates to the 13th century.

Mudéjar arches in the Sinagoga de Santa María la Blanca

Monasterio de San Juan de los Reyes

Calle de los Reyes Católicos 17. Open daily except 1 Jan, 25 Dec. Adm charge.

This monastery retains features such as a Gothic cloister (1510) with multi-coloured Mudéjar ceiling.

VISITORS' CHECKLIST

Airport/railway station: Paseo de la Rosa. Tourist information: Puerta de Bisagra, Tel 92 522 08 43. Market: Tue. Festivals: Corpus Christi (May/Jun), Virgen del Sagrario (15 Aug). **www.toledo-turismo.com**

Museo del Greco

Paseo del Tránsito. Open Tue–Sat, Sun am. Adm charge. Free Sat pm, Sun am.

This museum is located in Toledo's Jewish Quarter. It includes El Greco's *View of Toledo* and the superb series *Christ and the Apostles*.

Iglesia de Santiago del Arrabal

Calle Real de Arrabal. Free.

This is one of Toledo's most beautiful Mudéjar monuments. It can easily be identified by its tower, reminiscent of a minaret.

Puerta Antigua de Bisagra

When Alfonso VI conquered Toledo in 1085, he entered it through this gateway, alongside El Cid.

STREET LIFE

RESTAURANTS

Hacienda del Cardenal

Paseo de Recaredo 24.
Tel 92 522 08 62.
Moderate

Once the summer residence of Cardinal Lorenzana, this 18th-century palace serves garlic soup, suckling pig and the famous Toledo mazapán *(marzipan).*

Mesón La Orza

Calle de Descalzos 5.
Tel 92 522 30 11.
Closed Sun pm.
Moderate

In the heart of the Jewish Quarter, this traditional inn serves local cuisine. The meat dishes are especially good.

See p80 for price codes.

Toledo Cathedral

The splendour of Toledo's massive cathedral, whose construction began in 1226 and spanned three centuries, reflects its history as the spiritual heart of the Spanish church and the seat of the Primate of all Spain.

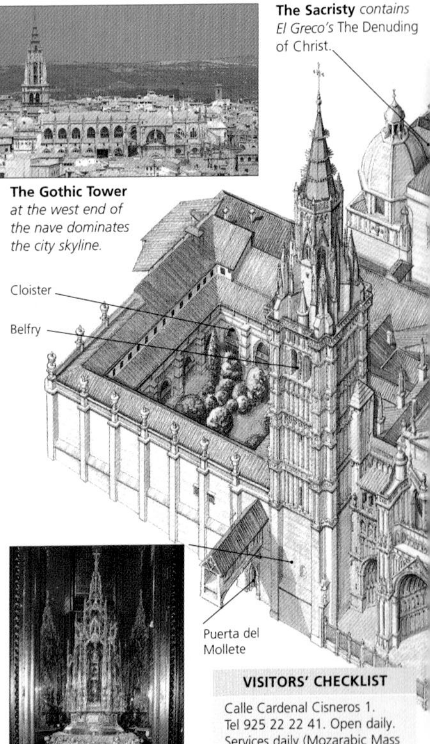

The Sacristy *contains El Greco's* The Denuding of Christ.

The Gothic Tower *at the west end of the nave dominates the city skyline.*

The Gothic Monstrance *is over 3 m (10 ft) high.*

VISITORS' CHECKLIST

Calle Cardenal Cisneros 1. Tel 925 22 22 41. Open daily. Services daily (Mozarabic Mass 9am Mon–Sat, 9:45am Sun). Choir, Treasury, Sacristy and Chapterhouse open 10am–6:30pm Mon–Sat, 2–6:30pm Sun. Adm charge. **www.catedralprimada.es**

The Transparente *is a Baroque altarpiece by Narciso Tomé.*

Capilla de San Ildefonso

Capilla de Santiago

The Chapterhouse *has a spectacular Mudéjar ceiling.*

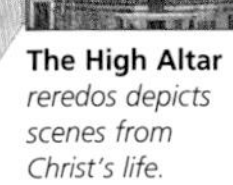

The High Altar *reredos depicts scenes from Christ's life.*

Puerta de los Leones

Puerta Llana entrance

Puerta del Perdón

The Choir *is decorated on the wooden lower stalls with scenes of the fall of Granada.*

Capilla Mozárabe

Getting Around

Most tourist sights are clustered together in the centre of Madrid, within walking distance of each other. Remember some museums and shops close 2–5pm. The Metro is the best way to travel around, but the city bus service is excellent, too.

Walking Tours in Madrid

Madrid a tu aire organizes daily walking tours in English – an informative and entertaining introduction to the city. Call 610 22 84 24 to book.

Cycling

Bicycle, moped or motorcycle helps in avoiding traffic and parking issues, but is only safe on Sundays and public holidays. The city is progressively adapting to bikers but crash helmets must be worn. Rent a bicycle from Bicimad (bicimad.com), the public bike rental service.

Driving

Madrileños drive aggressively, so be careful. Watch for one-way systems, tunnels and overpasses. Carry a valid driver's licence (an international one if not from the EU) and insurance documents. Traffic drives on the right, seat belts are compulsory for front-seat passengers and it's illegal to wear head-phones or to use mobile phone at the wheel.

Parking

If your hotel does not have parking, use an official underground car park (e.g. at Plaza Santa Ana, Plaza Mayor or Plaza de Oriente). A green sign (*libre*) means there is space, a red sign (*completo*) means full. Or park in a designated street area using the pay-and-display system: green lines mean a limit of one hour, blue lines no more than 2 hours.

No parking sign

Taxis

City taxis are white with a diagonal red stripe on the door and a green light on the roof. Hail them on the street or from a rank. They charge extra for luggage, airport pick-ups and on Sundays, public holidays and at night. Uber and Cabify are alternative options.

Tourist Card

The most practical and economical way to get around the city is to buy a tourist card, valid on all public transport. The card is non-transferable and can be purchased at all stations on the Metro network and headquarters of the Regional Transport Consortium Madrid. An official document must be presented whenever it is used.

Travelling by Metro

The quickest, cheapest and easiest way to get around the city, it is open from 6am–2am. Trains run every 3–5 minutes in peak hours. You will need to know the direction you're travelling in and the name of the end station.

Entrance of Lavapies Metro station

Travelling by Bus

Buses run from 6am until 11:30pm. Bus stops display bus numbers and routes. Pay the driver or use a Transport Card. Request a stop by pressing a button next to the exit doors. All night buses (*búhos*) leave from Plaza de Cibeles and run every half hour from midnight to 3am, then hourly until 6am, and every 20 minutes Fridays and Saturdays.

Bus Tours

The Madrid Tourist Bus is managed by the bus service *Empresa Municipal de Transportes* (EMT) from City Hall. There are two routes – historic Madrid and modern Madrid – and they run frequently between 9:30am–midnight in summer, 10am–7pm in winter (to 9pm in spring and autumn). The tours can be combined, and travellers can hop on and off at any stage.

The Madrid city tour bus

Travelling by Train

The Spanish national rail network, RENFE, has two long-distance train stations in Madrid: Atocha and Chamartín, linked by a tunnel. Trains stop at both stations and often the intermediate stations: Nuevos Ministerios and Recoletos. *Cercanías,* the suburban train network, is connected at various points to the Metro.

AVE trains at Atocha station

TRAVEL INFORMATION

EMT Bus Information
Tel: 90 250 78 50
Main Tourist Office
Plaza Mayor 27
Tel: 91 454 44 10
(Open 9:30am–8:30pm daily)
Metro Information
Tel: 90 244 44 03
RENFE Train Information
Tel: 90 232 03 20

Survival Guide

Madrid is a relatively safe city, but muggings can happen and pickpockets operate in crowds and at tourist sights. Take care when crossing the road: cars often jump red lights and pedestrians do not automatically have right of way on crossings.

Bureau de change

MONEY

Currency
The Spanish currency is the euro (€). Euro banknotes have seven denominations from €5 to €500 and eight coin denominations from 1 *céntimo* to €2.

Banks
Banks are open 8:30am–2pm Mon–Fri; some are open 9am–1pm on Sat, except in August. During the San Isidro festival all banks close at noon.

Credit Cards
In Madrid most hotels and restaurants take credit cards, but some pensions, *tabernas* and *tapas* bars will only accept cash.

Changing Money
Bureaux de change are found throughout Madrid. There are counters at Barajas airport, the two railway stations, big stores, major hotels and banks.

Cash Dispensers
ATMs abound in Madrid and are the easiest way of getting cash. Those that accept internationally recognized cards give a choice of several languages, including English.

Travellers' Cheques
Buy your cheques from AmEx (American Express), Travelex or your bank. All are accepted in Spain.

COMMUNICATIONS

Post Offices
The main office in Plaza de Cibeles is open 8:30am–9:30pm Mon–Fri, 8:30am–2pm on Sat. Smaller post offices, designated by a yellow sign and crown and post-horn logo, are open 8:30am–8:30pm Mon–Fri, to 1pm on Sat. You can also buy stamps at a tobacconist (*estanco*), designated by a brown-and-yellow sign.

Telephones
Both public telephone boxes (*cabinas*) and payphones in bars take coins. Some public telephones accept phonecards, on sale at post offices, newsstands and tobacconists

Movistar logo

(*estancos*). Only a few take credit cards. In telephone offices (*locutorios*), you make your call and pay for it later. The cheapest are run by Movistar (Telefónica). Madrid phone numbers start with 91, followed by seven digits.

Internet Cafés

These can be found all over Madrid. Workcenter (at Paseo de la Castellana 149) is open daily, and offers printing, binding and courier services.

HEALTH AND SAFETY

Travel Safety Advice

Visitors can get up-to-date travel safety information from the Foreign and Commonwealth Office (UK), the State Department (US) and the Department of Foreign Affairs and Trade (Australia).

Police

Stations in central Madrid are listed in the *Yellow Pages* (*Páginas Amarillas*). Central Police Station is at Calle Leganitos 19, tel: 91 548 79 85. Remember to report all crimes for insurance purposes. Keep copies of statements you make to the police and contact the Foreign Office Tourist Assistance Service (SATE), tel: 902 102 112.

Health and Insurance

All EU visitors should obtain a European Health Insurance Card before leaving home. Non-EU visitors must have medical cover.

Hospitals and Ambulances

In a medical emergency, go to the casualty departments (*Urgencias*) at:

- Hospital General Gregorio Marañón, Calle Dr Esquerdo 46, tel: 91 586 80 00; or
- Hospital La Paz, Paseo de la Castellana 261, tel: 91 727 70 00.

Other hospitals are listed in the *Yellow Pages* by area. For English-speaking doctors and dentists, contact:

- Anglo-American Medical Unit, Calle Conde de Aranda 1, tel: 91 435 18 23.

If you need an ambulance urgently, dial the city service (SAMUR) on 092, or:

- Red Cross Ambulances (*Ambulancias de la Cruz Roja*), tel: 91 522 22 22; or the emergency number.

Dentists

Ask your hotel for the nearest dentist or consult the *Yellow Pages*. For 24-hour emergencies, contact:

- Urgencias Dentales, Calle Bretón de los Herreros 32, tel: 91 441 41 84.

Pharmacies

An illuminated red or green cross designates a pharmacy (*farmacia*), many open 10am–8:30pm Mon–Sat. Notices in the window will say which pharmacies are open outside normal hours.

EMERGENCY NUMBERS

Ambulance
Tel: 061

Police
Tel: 091

Municipal Police
Tel: 092

General Emergencies
Tel: 112

Travel Safety Advice
Australia: www.dfat.gov.au
www.smartraveller.gov.au
UK: www.gov.uk/foreign-traveladvice
US: www.travel.state.gov

Index

Alcalá de Henares 66
Alfonso XII 27, 35
architecture 6
Art Deco architecture 6, 9, 13
Azca 48

Banco de España 29
Barca, Calderón de la 12
Baroque architecture 6, 44
Berrocol 43
bars and cafés
- Bodega de Angel Sierra 5
- in Bourbon Madrid 37
- Café Gijón 40
- in La Castellana 45
- in Old Madrid 25
- La Pecera café 32
- in Segovia 65
- Taberna de Antonio Sánchez 7, 25
- Viva Madrid 7, 25

Basílica Pontificia de San Miguel 11
La Bola 7, 25
Bolsa de Comercio 30
Botín 7, 25
Bourbon architecture 6
Buitrago del Lozoya 60

Café Gijón 40
CaixaForum 33
Calle del Almirante 40
Calle de Preciados 16
Calle de Serrano 42
The Calvary 55
Campo del Moro 7, 23
Capitol building 9
Carlos V 70
Casa de Lope de Vega 33
Casa de la Panaderia 10
Catedral de la Almudena 23
Cervantes, Miguel de 16, 41, 66
Chinchón 66, 67
El Cid 35
Círculo de Bellas Artes 32
Colegiata de San Isidro 11
Colegio de San Ildefonso (Alcalá de Henares) 66
Columbus, Christopher 4, 42
La Corrala 50
Cuartel del Conde Duque 45

desornamentado architecture 55
El Doncel 61

Edificio Metrópolis 32
Ermita de San Antonio de la Florida 51
El Escorial 54–7
- The Basílica 57
- Chapterhouses 56
- The Library 54, 57
- The Museums 55, 57
- Palace of the Bourbons 57
- Palacio de los Austrias 56
- Pantheons 54, 56
- Royal Apartments 56
- Salas Capitulares 56

Estación de Atocha 7, 37
Estación de Príncipe Pío 51

Felipe IV 22
Fuente de Cibeles 29
Fundación Juan March 43

Giordano, Luca 55, 57
The Glory of the Spanish Monarchy 55
Gran Vía 4, 6, 9, 13, 14–15
La Granja de San Ildefonso 60
El Greco 53, 71, 72
Guadalajara 61
Guernica 6, 37

Habsburg architecture 6, 12
Hotel Ritz 30
Iglesia de San Jerónimo el Real 35
Iglesia de San José 32
Iglesia de San Nicolás 23
Iglesia de San Plácido 45
Iglesia de Santa Bárbara 40, 41
Illescas 67

Kilometre Zero 10

La Latina 24

Madrid a tu aire 74
Malasaña 44, 45
Manzanares el Real 58
Matadero Madrid 49
Mercado de San Miguel 10, 11
Ministerio de Agricultura 36
Mirador del Faro 48
Monasterio de las Descalzas Reales 6, 16
Monasterio de la Encarnación 17
Monasterio de Santa Maria de El Paular 59
Muralla Árabe 24
Museo del Aire 66
Museo de América 48
Museo Arqueológico Nacional 6, 42
Museo Casa de la Moneda 49
Museo de Cera 41
Museo de Ciencias Naturales 48, 49
Museo del Ferrocarril 50
Museo de Historia de Madrid 6, 44
Museo Lázaro Galdiano 43
Museo Nacional de Antropología 36
Museo Nacional de Artes Decorativas 30
Museo Naval 29
Museo del Prado 6, 7, 34
Museo Reina Sofía (MNCARS) 5, 6, 37
Museo del Romanticismo 44
Museo del Traje 48
Museo Sorolla 44

Museo Thyssen-Bornemisza 6, 31

Navacerrada Pass 59
Neo-Classical architecture 6

Palacio de Comunicaciones 29
Palacio de los Duques del Infantado 61
Palacio de Fernán Núñez 37
Palacio de Linares 28
Palacio de Liria 45
Palacio de El Pardo 66
Palacio Real 6, 18–21, 23
 Armoury 21
 Carlos III Rooms 18, 20
 Chapel Rooms 21
 Dining Room 18, 21
 Entrance Rooms 19, 20
 The Palace 20
 Pharmacy 21
 Plaza de Armas 20, 21
Palacio Real de Aranjuez 7, 67
Palacio de Santa Cruz 12
Palacio del Senado 17
Parque del Retiro 7, 27, 35
La Pecera café 32
Picasso 6, 37
Plaza de Armas 21
Plaza del Callao 13
Plaza de Chueca 5, 40
Plaza de Cibeles 5, 29
Plaza de Colón 4, 39, 42
Plaza de España 13, 16
Plaza Mayor 4, 10
Plaza Mayor (Chinchón) 67
Plaza de Oriente 22
Plaza de la Paja 24
Plaza de Santa Ana 12
Plaza de Toros de Las Ventas 47, 49
Plaza de la Villa 11
Puente de Segovia 50
Puerta de Alcalá 6, 28
Puerta del Sol 10
Puerta de Toledo 50

El Rastro 24
Real Academia de Bellas Artes de San Fernando 12
Real Academia Española 35
Real Fábrica de Tapices 50
Real Jardín Botánico 7, 36
Real Observatorio Astronómico de Madrid 36
restaurants
 La Bola 7, 25
 in Bourbon Madrid 37
 in La Castellana 45
 in Old Madrid 25
 in Segovia 65
 El Sobrino del Botin 7, 25
 in Toledo 71
de Ribera, Pedro 44
Río Manzanares 50

Sala del Canal de Isabel II 48
Salamanca 42
Salamanca, Marqués de 43
San Francisco el Grande 24
Santa Cruz del Valle de los Caídos 58
Segovia 62–5
 Alcázar 63, 64
 Aqueduct 64
 Casa de los Picos 64
 Cathedral 62
 Iglesia de San Millán 65
 Iglesia de la Vera Cruz 65
 Monasterio de los Carmelitas 65
 Monasterio de El Parral 65
 Museo de Segovia 62
 Palacio Episcopal 64
 Plaza Mayor 65
 San Esteban 65
 San Juan de los Caballeros 65
 San Martin 65
shopping
 in La Castellana 45
 Mercado de San Miguel 10, 11
 in Old Madrid 25
 in El Rastro 24
Sierra Centro de Guadarrama 58, 59
Sierra Norte 61
Sigüenza 61
Sorolla, Joaquin 44
Stock Exchange 30

Taberna de Antonio Sánchez 7, 25
Teatro Español 33
Teatro Real 22
Telefónica 13
Templo de Debod 51
La Tizona (sword) 35
Toledo 68–73
 Alcázar 70
 Iglesia de Santiago del Arrabal 71
 Iglesia de Santo Tomé 70
 Monasterio de San Juan de los Reyes 71
 Museo de Santa Cruz 70
 Museo del Greco 53, 71
 Puerta Antigua de Bisagra 71
 Sinagoga de Santa María la Blanca 71
 Sinagoga del Tránsito 70
 Toledo Cathedral 72–3
Tomé, Narciso 73
The Transparente 73
Tribunal Supremo 41

van der Weyden, Rogier 55, 57
La Venencia 7, 25
Viva Madrid 7, 25

Westin Palace 30

Acknowledgments

Dorling Kindersley would like to thank the following people whose help and assistance contributed to the preparation of this book.

Design and Editorial

Publisher Douglas Amrine
Publishing Manager Vivien Antwi
Managing Art Editor Kate Poole
Cartography Casper Morris
Design Maite Lantaron
Production Controller Shane Higgins
Picture Research Ellen Root
DTP Jason Little
Jacket Design Tessa Bindloss

Revisions Team Cristina Barrallo, Emma Brady, Paula Canal, Neha Chander, Samantha Cook, Caroline Elliker, Aishwarya Gosain, Lydia Halliday, Claire Jones, Bharti Karakoti, Sumita Khatwani, Rahul Kumar, Jude Ledger, Candela Madaria, Alison McGill, Caroline Mead, Sonal Modha, Marianne Petrou, Andrea Pinnington, Mani Ramaswamy, Marisa Renzullo, Beverly Smart, Avantika Sukhia, Priyanka Thakur, Ajay Verma, Hugo Wilkinson, Word on Spain.

Picture Credits

Key:
a-above; b-below/bottom; c-centre; f-far; l-left; r-right; t-top.

The Publishers are grateful to the following individuals, companies and picture libraries for permission to reproduce their photographs:

Alamy Images: Age fotostock 32t, John Kellerman 18cl.
Alamy Stock Photo: Richard Bradley 40cr.

Corbis: Macduff Everton 35tr, Jon Hicks 8.

Dreamstime.com: Ahkenahmed 26, Americanspirit 34tl, Digitalsignal 16br, Epalaciosan 5crb, Isaías Ibáñez 59t, Vichaya Kiatying-angsulee 13bl, Karol Kozlowski 51tr, Maksershov 11t, Milosk50 49b, Eq Roy 75cl, Svetlana195 22tl, 75bl Robert Zehetmayer 10cr.

Robert Harding Picture Library: James Strachan 17b, 51b.
Anthony King: 76t.

La Casa del Abuelo: 3cr

Museo Nacional Centro de Arte Reina Sofia, Madrid: 37cr.

National Atesa: 74b

Prisma, Barcelona: 24bl.

Real Academia Española 33br

Archivio del Senado: Oronoz 17cl.

Telefónica: 77tl.

Jacket
Front – Corbis: dpa/Matthias Schrader t.
Back – Dorling Kindersley: Rough Guides/Ian Aitken t.
All other images © Dorling Kindersley

For further information see www.DKimages.com.

Price Codes are for a three-course meal per person including half a bottle of wine (or equivalent meal), taxes and extra charges
Cheap under €25
Moderate €25–€55
Expensive €55 or more

Phrase Book

In Emergency

Help!	**¡Socorro!**	soh-**koh**-roh
Stop!	**¡Pare!**	**pah**-reh
Call a doctor!	**¡Llame a un médico!**	**yah**-meh ah **oon meh**-dee-koh
Call an ambulance!	**¡Llame a una ambulancia!**	**yah**-meh ah **oonah** ahm-boo-**lahn**-thee-ah
Call the police!	**¡Llame a la policía!**	**yah**-meh ah lah poh-lee-**thee**-ah
Call the fire brigade!	**¡Llame a los bomberos!**	**yah**-meh ah lohs bohm-**beh**-rohs
Where is the nearest telephone?	**¿Dónde está el teléfono más próximo?**	**dohn**-deh ehs-**tah** ehl teh-**leh**-foh-noh **mahs prohx**-ee-moh
Where is the nearest hospital?	**¿Dónde está el hospital más próximo?**	**dohn**-deh ehs-**tah** ehl ohs-pee-**tahl mahs prohx**-ee-moh

Communication Essentials

Yes	**Sí**	see
No	**No**	noh
Please	**Por favor**	pohr fah-**vohr**
Thank you	**Gracias**	**grah**-thee-ahs
Excuse me	**Perdone**	pehr-**doh**-neh
Hello	**Hola**	**oh**-lah
Goodbye	**Adiós**	ah-dee-**ohs**

Useful Phrases

How are you?	**¿Cómo está usted?**	**koh**-moh ehs-**tah** oos-**tehd**
Very well, thank you.	**Muy bien, gracias.**	mwee bee-**ehn grah**-thee-ahs
Pleased to meet you.	**Encantado de conocerle.**	ehn-kahn-**tah**-doh deh koh-noh-**thehr**-leh
That's fine.	**Está bien.**	ehs-**tah** bee-**ehn**
Where is/are . . .?	**¿Dónde está/están . . .?**	**dohn**-deh ehs-**tah**/ehs-**tahn**
How far is it to . . .?	**Cuántos metros/ kilómetros hay de aquí a . . .?**	**kwahn**-tohs **meh**-trohs/kee-**loh**-meh-trohs **eye** deh ah-**kee** ah
Which way to . . .?	**¿Por dónde se va a . . .?**	pohr **dohn**-deh seh **bah** ah
Do you speak English?	**¿Habla inglés?**	**ah**-blah een-**glehs**
I don't understand	**No comprendo**	noh kohm-**prehn**-doh
Could you speak more slowly please?	**¿Puede hablar más despacio por favor?**	pweh-deh ah-**blahr mahs** dehs-pah-thee-oh pohr fah-**vohr**

Useful Words

big	**grande**	**grahn**-deh
small	**pequeño**	peh-**keh**-nyoh
hot	**caliente**	kah-lee-**ehn**-teh
cold	**frío**	**free**-oh
open	**abierto**	ah-bee-**ehr**-toh
closed	**cerrado**	thehr-**rah**-doh
left	**izquierda**	eeth-key-**ehr**-dah
right	**derecha**	deh-**reh**-cha
straight on	**todo recto**	toh-doh **rehk**-toh
entrance	**entrada**	ehn-**trah**-dah